TRACK
AND
FIELD

TRACK
AND
FIELD

Secrets of the Champions

by GEORGE SULLIVAN
with photographs by the author

Doubleday & Company, Inc. Garden City, New York

Library of Congress Cataloging in Publication Data

Sullivan, George, 1927-
  Track and field.

  Includes index.
  SUMMARY: Presents basic instructions for performing
in various track and field events and tips from champions,
record holders, and other specialists.
  1. Track-athletics—Juvenile literature. 2. Track-
athletics—United States—Records—Juvenile literature.
3. Track and field athletes—United States—Biography—
Juvenile literature. [1. Track and field] I. Title.
GV1060.5.S92   796.4'2'0922 [B]
ISBN 0-385-14999-9 Trade
       0-385-15000-8 Prebound
Library of Congress Catalog Card Number 79-7508
9 8 7 6 5 4 3

Acknowledgments

The author is grateful to the many people who worked toward making this book possible, in particular the athletes who contributed instructional tips. Special thanks are also due John Devaney, editor, *The New American Runner;* Pete Cava, Amateur Athletic Union; Armand Laurino, Fordham Prep; Ed Robinson, Iona Relays; Gary Wagner, Wagner-International Photos; Herb Field, Herb Field Art Studio; Ed Friel, Aime LaMontagne, and Bill Sullivan.

Contents

1

Getting Started

Who can run the fastest? Who can jump the highest? Who can throw the farthest?

Many millions of men and women, and boys and girls — more Americans than ever before — are seeking to answer these questions.

If you are one of these track and field athletes, or are planning on becoming one, this book is meant for you. It not only presents basic instructional information concerning the various events, but it also gives tips — "secrets" — from noted champions, record holders, and other specialists.

There are many reasons for the widespread popularity and mushrooming growth of track and field. One coach explained it in these terms: "It means involvement," he said. "It's meeting people and having fun."

Having fun is very important. A surprising number of athletes I spoke with in preparing this book stressed that fact. Having fun also has practical value. When you're enjoying yourself, you're much more likely to do your best.

You can begin training and competing in most track and field events at an early age. Indeed, when it comes to running, young people often have better form than adults. Their strides are effortless. They keep their backs straight. They hold their arms at about waist level. And they do all of these things naturally. Dr. George Sheehan, a well-known expert on the subject of running, advises adults to study the way ten-year-old girls run. They often have *perfect* form, Dr. Sheehan says.

CHOOSING A SPECIALTY

When you're choosing an event in which to specialize, your age is not as an important factor as your particular physical characteristics. If you're tall and slender, you'll probably do your best in the running and jumping events. If you're on the stocky side, you're likely to excel in the field events, perhaps the shot put or the discus throw.

There are other factors to consider. A sprinter must have lightning-quick reflexes, the ability to explode away at the sound of the starter's pistol. A middle-distance runner has to have quick reflexes, be a speedster, and also have good stamina. With a distance runner, the emphasis is less on speed and more on endurance. If you're a distance runner, you also have to have the temperament that allows you to endure the long, often lonely hours of training.

To be a jumper, whether you're jumping for height or for distance, you need strong legs, especially in the thigh area. You need to be fast, too, having almost a sprinter's speed. You need to be taller than average, especially for the high jump.

Such standards are not rigidly fixed, however. Houston McTear, acknowledged to be the best sprinter in the United States during late 1970s, had a blocky build. And Franklin Jacobs, who set the indoor high-jumping record in 1978 with a leap of 7'7¼", was not considered particularly tall for a college athlete, standing 5'8½". (Jacobs claimed to hold the world record for inches jumped above one's height: 23¼".)

Also be aware that simply because you choose one event or one category of events, you don't necessarily have to remain in that category for all time. You can change. Indeed,

Martha Cooksey—"Don't overwork; enjoy yourself."

Martha Cooksey
Orange, California

1978 Woman Road Runner of the Year, Track and Field News
1978 AAU Women's Marathon Champion (2:41.55)

If you want to have a long career in running, be careful about your training. Don't overwork. Enjoy yourself. Too many young runners burn themselves out mentally and physically. Make training fun. Be creative about what you do. Get off the track; get off the asphalt. Run in parks or on cross-country courses. Take one-way running trips to different places. The motivation for running has to come from inside. If you're not enjoying it, you won't be motivated.

as you enter your late teens or early twenties, your physical characteristics can change. So you may not only want to change, your "new" height and weight may make changing something of a necessity.

If you're like most track and field athletes, you'll start competing when you're in grade school, junior high, or high school. But there are many other opportunities for competition, especially on a pre-high school basis.

The Road Runners Club Sponsors cross-country championships and other events for boys and girls beginning at age six and seven and on through high school. These are "age-group" races, which means you'll be competing against youngsters who are the same age as you are.

The Amateur Athletic Union (the AAU) offers a nationwide Junior Olympics program that is growing by leaps and bounds. Like the Road Runners program, its competition is on an age-group basis. The AAU's rival, the U.S. Track and Field Federation, sponsors a program of its own called Junior Champs.

For information about these programs, write to each of the organizations. Their addresses are listed in the Appendix.

Once you become interested in track and field, you may be perplexed by the fact that running events are sometimes designated in meters and other times in yards and miles. (Conversion tables are to be found in the Appendix of this book.) There is a trend toward changing over to a fully metric system, but until the switch has been completed some confusion will be normal.

The 200-meter dash, for example, is replacing the 220-yard event on every level of competition. The same is true of 400 meters as opposed to 440 yards, and 800 meters vs. 800 yards. Even the mile, a sacred distance in the United States, is beginning to be supplanted by the 1,500 meter race. The best evidence of this is the marked decrease in the number of four-minute milers. In one recent year, only eleven Americans ran sub-4:00 miles. But twenty-three American runners bettered the equivalent time for 1,500 meters, which is 3:42.2.

One other point must be mentioned. It has to do with

some of the records cited in this book and the manner in which performances related to those records were timed. Automatically timed performances may be listed as "records" even though there are faster hand-timed marks. Hand timing produced faster marks because the timer reacted to the flash of the starter's gun, and hence there was a delay.

But automatic timers are wired to the gun itself, and start recording simultaneously. In addition, the finish is recorded by an automatic camera. As a result, the new automatically timed records may be as much as one-tenth of a second "slower" than the old marks. At some point in the future, only automatically timed records will be recognized in the sprints.

FOOTWEAR

When you run a mile, each of your running shoes strikes the ground about 1,000 times. If you run a mile five or six times a week, that means each shoe strikes the ground about 250,000 in a year. That statistic makes it clear why good running shoes are important.

If you're new to track and field, the enormous variety of

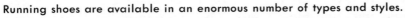

Running shoes are available in an enormous number of types and styles.

running shoes available today can't help but bewilder you. Nevertheless, you must take the time to pick out a shoe that fits you perfectly and is best suited for the events you plan to enter. The proper shoes can make a big difference in your performance.

Most of the better running shoes are made in foreign countries. The Dassler brothers of West Germany were pioneers in the field. One of the Dasslers founded the Adidas Company. Another Dassler formed Puma.

Later, Tiger and Nike, both Japanese firms, entered the field. There is also Pony from Canada, Patrick from France, Reebok from England, and Karhu from Finland. American Manufacturers are represented by New Balance, Converse, Brooks, and Eaton.

Most track and field athletes nowadays own two kinds of shoes. One pair is for competitive running. Competition shoes are either spikes or racing flats (which are lightweight shoes without spikes). The other pair is for training. They're called training flats.

Don't confuse training or racing flats with sneakers. Most sneakers have little or no arch support and are not sufficiently padded inside. Your feet need to be cushioned and protected, and sneakers, for the most part, fail to provide these necessities.

Flats cover a wide range as far as their weight is concerned. In fact, weight is one of the chief differences between training flats and racing flats. The last named have to be very light. Frank Shorter, Olympic gold medalist in the marathon in 1972, tells about one competitor who stayed up all night before the race shaving milligrams from his shoes to make them lighter. A milligram doesn't mean much—it's about equal in weight to a small puff of smoke—but an ounce can make a difference. Think of it in these terms: you take almost 2,000 steps in a mile. In a mile run, that means being burdened by lifting 2,000 extra ounces, or 125 pounds. Thus, if your training program is going to include a good deal of distance running, be wary of heavier-than-normal training flats.

Whether you're buying spikes or flats, certain fundamen-

Marty Liquori — "Padding is what you should look for . . ."

Marty Liquori
Gainesville, Florida

World-Class Miler (3:52.2, 1975)
AAU Champion, 1,500 Meters, 1969 (3:59.5), 1971 (3:56.5)

When buying shoes, a lot of kids make the mistake of sacrificing padding for lightness. But padding is what you should look for. A lightweight shoe doesn't give the cushioning or support a young runner needs. If you do buy lightweight shoes, don't wear tham all the time, only when you're going to compete.

Make sure you get the right fit, of course. Remember that shoe sizes are different among different shoe companies. What's a size 9½ for one company isn't necessarily a 9½ for another. Go by how the shoe feels on your foot. There should be plenty of space for your toes. Your feet swell when you run, so you have to allow for this. There should be at least a half an inch of space between the end of toes and the end of the shoe. Put a finger there and press down. There should be space there about equal to the width of your finger.

Be sure the sole is bendable.

tals apply. The sole of the shoe should not only give you the traction you're looking for, but it should be flexible, too. If it's stiff, you can't bend your foot properly. Take the shoe in both hands, gripping at the heel end with one hand, the toe end with the other. Then double the sole in half. It should bend easily. If it doesn't, it may be too stiff for running.

At the same time, you want a sole that's thick enough and tough enough to cushion your foot on each stride. To deliver all of these benefits, the shoe is likely to have a sole that consists of a rugged outer layer and one or two softer inner layers.

In training and racing flats, check to see that the heel is elevated, particularly if distance running is going to be your specialty. This method of construction serves to lessen the strain on your legs when you run.

Inspect the inside of the shoe. There should be no seams, nothing that can cause irritation to your foot. The insole of the shoe, the surface upon which the foot rests, should be soft yet offer plenty of support.

The heel counter, a solid piece of rubber or synthetic material at the back of the shoe, should aid in giving stability to your foot. There should be padding at the ankle and on the inside of the tongue.

The upper is that part of the shoe above the sole. Uppers are what give the shoes their distinctive appearance. Many people buy shoes because of the color of the uppers, plus the manufacturer's striping or symbol that is blazoned on the side. Forget about color; forget about the manufacturer's emblem. Instead, evaluate uppers on the basis of function. Do they stabilize your feet? Is the material soft enough so it's not going to cause any chafing? What kind of material are the uppers made of? The best running shoes are made of nylon and leather. Either one is recommended, although nylon has a slight edge. It's light in weight, allows plenty of air to circulate, and is easier to clean. Nylon shoes can be tossed into a washing machine and not be harmed,

Treads are one of the most distinctive features of running shoes. During the mid-1970s, the Nike Company introduced the "waffle" tread, a series of raised grippers meant to provide better traction. They were intended for use on soft surfaces — on grass and dirt paths. But it wasn't long before shoe experts and the public in general became convinced that they worked just as well on concrete and asphalt as they did on the ground. Now, every manufacturer has shoes of this type. Since the original square waffle pattern is patented by Nike, the other manufacturers must offer variations — round-, triangular-, or star-shaped patterns.

The shape of the individual grippers that make up the tread isn't a critical matter. You do, however, have to be wary of grippers that are too long and too thin. Shoes with grippers of this type may shimmy when you run on a hard surface, an effect that feels something like a skateboard with a loose wheel. Look for short, broad grippers, with a pattern in which the individual nibs are close together.

When you run in shoes with waffle treads, the impact of each stride is cushioned by the grippers rather than by the foot as a whole, which is the case with solid-soled shoes. At least, that's what the manufacturers of these shoes claim. Experts who have conducted laboratory tests on waffle-tread shoes will only say that these claims are "probably true." It boils down to personal preference. If you like waffle treads, wear them.

Flats should fit snugly, but they shouldn't pinch. Women often need smaller and narrower shoes than men. Up until a few years ago, they had to buy men's shoes, and often they didn't fit very well. But now the leading shoe manufacturers offer training and racing flats in women's sizes.

One way to assure you'll get a proper fit is to first make an outline drawing of your foot. Simply place each foot on a piece of paper and draw around it. Don't merely do one foot; do both. It's very likely your left foot is a bit longer than your right, or vice versa. When you go shopping for shoes, take the outline drawings with you. Compare the bottom of each shoe to the tracings. Are the shoes long enough? Are they wide enough across the ball of the foot and in the toe area?

The toe area is especially important. When you run, each foot in turn slides forward inside the shoe, so you need some extra room there. Allow from $1/2$ to $3/4$ inch between your toes and the front of the shoe. If you don't have sufficient room in the toe area, soreness and then blisters are almost certain to be the result.

The heel of the shoe should hold the heel of your foot snugly, with the counter hitting the back of your foot at a comfortable level. If it's too high, it can chafe and cause blisters. If it's too low, it's not likely to give you the support you need.

Some runners encounter a problem because the front of their foot is extra wide in proportion to the back. The result is that their heel swims around inside the back of the shoe. To remedy this condition, tape a strip of felt or foam rubber along the sides toward the back of the shoe. Don't do the taping at the back of the heel; tape there can cause blisters.

Much of what's said above applies to spikes, too. The type of spikes you wear depends to a great extent on your specialty. Sprinters' shoes have six or seven spikes arranged in an oval pattern near the outer edges of the sole. There are no heel spikes because sprinters run only on their toes.

A middle-distance shoe may have two or three spikes placed near the arch area, the others closer to the toe. High jumpers have two spikes in each heel because they plant a heel just before they jump.

When you're buying spiked shoes, be sure that the front spikes are positioned just behind the front part of the big toe. The back spikes should be no farther forward than the arch of your foot.

The length of the spikes is another important consideration, although you don't have to make a decision about spike length in the shoe store. Quality shoes have screw-in spikes. You simply replace one length with another whenever you want.

The length to use depends upon the type of surface on which you're competing. For indoor tracks or outdoors on

Quality racing flats have interchangeable spikes.

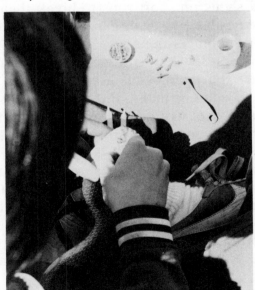

what are called all-weather surfaces, short spikes are used. These are spikes that are no longer than 6 mm. Some coaches are now recommending short spikes with star-shaped heads, instead of the traditional nail heads or cone-shaped heads. Since the star head does not pierce the track surface, it does not have to be pulled out on each stride, and the result is a saving in running energy.

Middle-distance runners usually wear longer spikes than sprinters, although the nature of the surface still must be considered. A middle-distance runner might wear 12 mm spikes in front, 15 mm spikes in back.

Javelin throwers put tremendous strain on their legs and feet as they brake their forward motion and seek to transfer their momentum to their upper body and throwing arm. To help withstand this pressure, they wear very long spikes, sometimes longer than those of any other athlete.

Spikes are not important to shot putters and discus throwers. But they have to have strong, tight fitting shoes. The shot putter has to be able to glide backward across the throwing circle as he prepares to release, and spikes could prevent him from executing this move. Spikes could also be detrimental to the discus thrower as he winds up and releases.

You should always purchase new shoes before the old ones are completely worn out. Then you'll have a chance to wear the new shoes on short runs to break them in. By the time the old shoes have to be discarded, the new ones will be ready to wear in competition.

Some runners develop an affection for a certain pair of shoes and hate the thought of discarding them. They may even feel the shoes to be lucky. But be careful about running in worn shoes. A heel worn down by as little as a quarter of an inch can change your running form, and cause leg soreness as a result.

You can solve the problem of wear by patching shoe soles with any one of several kinds of liquid coatings sold in tubes and available at shoe repair shops. They have names such as "Shoe Patch" and "Shoe Goo."

It's important to start applying the coating at the first sign of wear. If too much of the shoe material has been ground away, it's difficult to do an efficient repair job. Think in terms of wearing out the coating, not shoe material.

Always apply the coating in very thin layers, being careful to keep the original contour of the sole. A thick blob of patching material at the heel can cause an imbalance that is just as harmful as a worn heel.

Some shoe repair shops specialize in resoling running shoes. The reasons that runners get shoes resoled are economic. The cost of a resoling job is about one-third the price of a new pair of shoes. But be cautious about having shoes resoled. The shoes you get back are not going to be exactly like the shoes you handed in. After all, they're going to be rebuilt, and even the size can be different. Before you decide to have running shoes resoled, check with other runners about their experiences with the repair shop you intend to use. Even if you consider your shoes to be exceptionally lucky, it's usually better to buy new ones.

Running shoes of the future may make shoes of the present day seem primitive by comparison. At least one manufacturer is working on an inflatable shoe. You slip it on and then fill it up with air (from an aerosol can). Such a shoe will be much lighter and very efficient in cushioning the foot. Blisters may become a thing of the past. There won't even be shoelaces to tie, the laces being replaced by an elastic band. The 1980s may see the introduction of inflatable running shoes.

Whether you wear socks is a matter of personal preference. Lightweight running shoes can be worn without socks. But if you have soft skin and your feet tend to get sore in spots and blister, socks can reduce the irritation. Socks also help absorb perspiration, which may be a factor if you're running over long distances. Socks are also recommended if you're running on a cinder track, for they can prevent cinder granules that get inside your shoes from embedding themselves in your feet.

RUNNING CLOTHING

For years, runners asked only that their shorts and tops be

loose fitting and comfortable. They're more demanding nowadays. They look for clothes made of "breathing" fabrics — those that let the body regulate its own heat, allowing moisture to evaporate through a layer of ventilated fabric, often mesh or fishnet. No longer does the runner have to get wet or clammy, even when covering a long distance.

Weight is another factor. A sleeveless competition shirt, designed by marathoner Frank Shorter, Olympic gold medalist in 1972, is made in two parts. The upper part, made of soft, lightweight nylon tricot, prevents chafing. The lower part is fishnet. The shirt weighs 3.04 ounces. (A standard T-shirt weighs about 4½ ounces.) Shorts designed by Shorter, with attached underpants, weigh .16 ounces more than the shorts, or 3.2 ounces.

Having shorts that are loose fitting is still of overriding importance, no matter how much they might happen to weigh. After trying on a pair of shorts, stand and raise one knee as high as you can. If the material binds across the top of your thigh, the shorts aren't loose enough.

You also need a track suit, also referred to as a warm-up suit, sweat suit, or, simply, sweats. A track suit must keep you warm before and after your events or warm-up session. The least expensive suits are made of cotton and, traditionally, are gray in color. You can also buy fancy velour or doubleknit outfits, and recently suits of lightweight downproof nylon have been introduced.

If you're going to be competing frequently, you should have several changes of clothing. Suppose you're competing in more than one event in one day; then bring two outfits with you and change between events. Not only will you look better, but fresh clothing tends to give an athlete a psychological boost.

For many years, Dr. Joan Ullyot, women's editor of *Runner's World* magazine, urged the development of a special bra for women runners. Manufacturers were listening. By the late 1970s, about a dozen of them were offering sports bras, among them Formfit, Rogers, Lily of France, and

Frank Shorter glides along in his lightweight running gear.

Danskin. These bras are light in weight and seamless, or have outside seams. No hooks or fasteners touch the skin.

YOUR DIET

If you're serious about track and field, you'll watch what you eat. Always eat three meals a day, striving for a well-balanced diet, one that provides proteins, carbohydrates, fats, and cellulose. Each of these has a purpose.

Protein — found in meat, fish, eggs, and cheese — contains carbon, hydrogen, oxygen, and nitrogen, which contribute to body growth and the repair of worn tissue.

Carbohydrates — found in sugar, potato, fruits, rice, pasta, and bread — contain carbon, hydrogen, and oxygen, and supply the body with energy.

Fats — found in butter, margarine, vegetable oils, and certain meats — provide carbon, hydrogen, and oxygen, which combine to form glycerol, and this supplies energy in great quantities. But you should keep a check on the amount of fats you consume.

Cellulose — found in fruits and vegetables — is a carbohydrate that aids in the movement of food through the digestive system.

Before you compete in an event, what you eat takes on added importance. Your body needs carbohydrates and fats for fuel. Up until a few years ago, many coaches would recommend eating a big steak before an event. Not any more. Meat is largely protein, which takes a relatively long time to digest. Protein-rich foods should not be consumed for at least seven or eight hours before a race. Instead, eat foods that are noted for their carbohydrates. On the evening before the Boston Marathon, more than a few of the city's restaurants offer special "all-you-can-eat spaghetti dinners" for runners who are loading up on carbohydrates in preparation for their long ordeal the next day. Pancake dinners are also popular.

Stay away from so called "junk foods," not only the day

before a race but as a general rule. As Steve Riddick, one of the outstanding spinters of recent times, once noted, "You eat a hamburger, you run like a hamburger."

WARMING UP

Before competition or any training session, you must warm up your body. Your warm-up drills should have two goals: first, to stimulate blood circulation; second, to stretch the muscles that you're going to be using.

Stimulating blood circulation is important because it's the blood that carries oxygen throughout the body. When the muscles perform heavy work, as in running, they burn up body fuels in combination with oxygen. If the muscles don't get the oxygen they require for their energy-producing role, painful spasms or cramps can be the result.

Track and field athletes usually begin their warm-up sessions with light jogging, maybe two laps around a quarter-mile track. Jogging increases the rate of blood circulation, but it does so slowly and gently. You should be sweating lightly when you've finished.

Next, perform your stretching exercises, focusing upon the muscles of the lower back, the calf muscles, the ham-

Begin your warm-up session with some light jogging.

strings (the tendons at the back of the knee), and the Achilles tendons (those at the back of the heel, joining the heel bone and the calf muscles).

How important are stretching exercises? Houston Mc-Tear, America's pre-eminent sprinter of recent years, knows. When McTear was a high school senior in Baker, Florida, a pulled right hamstring kept from competing in the 1976 Olympics, although he had qualified for the U. S. team. Not long after, McTear's training program began to be supervised by Larry McVey, who calls himself "a fanatic" for stretching. "When Houston came to me, he couldn't touch the floor with his hands," McVey once recalled. "His muscles were as hard as wood." McVey laid out a program of stretching exercises for Houston to follow. "Houston's muscles became more pliable, more maneuverable," McVey said. "He didn't have to worry about pulls." A healthy McTear was soon setting records in meet after meet.

The paragraphs that follow describe several different stretching exercises you can do. But don't look upon this as the ultimate list. Your coach or physical education instruction can give you many others.

Every exercise should be performed slowly, carefully, especially if you're a beginner. "Listen to your body," is what one coach says. If any exercise causes pain, don't do it, or modify it so you can do it without straining.

Sit-ups should be a regular part of your routine. Lie on your back, put your hands behind your head, then sit up, touching your right elbow to your left knee. Lie back down, then sit up again, touching the left elbow to the right knee. You may want to have a friend anchor your feet to the ground. At first, do 5 or 10 sit-ups. But you should be able to develop to a point where you're able to do 20 or 30 or more.

Leg lifts are another standard exercise. Lie on your back, your feet together, your hands at your side. Raise both legs about 6 inches, keeping your toes pointed toward the sky. Then spread your feet, and slowly bring them back together again. Lower your legs and repeat. You should be able to do this exercise 5 or 10 times.

DeAndra Carney—"Always stretch before you run."

DeAndra Carney
Los Angeles Mercurettes

U. S. Indoor Record, 60-yard dash, 1978 (6.72)

Always stretch before you run. Spend a half hour on it. Stretch those hamstrings especially.

Toe touches are good, too. Stand with your feet about shoulder-width apart and raise your arms above your head, as if you're reaching for the sky. Then bend from the waist, keeping your knees straight, and touch your toes with your fingertips. Stand erect and repeat. Do this exercise at least 10 times. Later, as the muscles of your back and at the back of your legs get stretched, your range of motion will increase, and you'll probably be able to touch your toes with your palms, or even put your palms to the ground in front of you.

An exercise known as the trunk twister is easy to do. Stand with your feet about shoulder width apart and put your hands on your hips. Face to the front and then twist your upper body to the left as far as you can; then twist it to the right. Then bend from the waist and repeat, first turning to the right and then the left. Do the exercise 10 times.

What's sometimes called the hurdler's exercise is performed by virtually every track and field athlete. Sit on the ground and open your legs as far as you can comfortably. Then double the right leg back, tucking the right foot beneath you. Place your hands on your left foot and then rock forward from the waist, attempting to touch your forehead to your

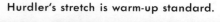
Hurdler's stretch is warm-up standard.

knee. Reverse the position of your legs and repeat. Do the exercise 5 times on each side.

The standing hamstring and calf muscle stretch is very popular. You have to have a vertical surface available in order to do it. A wall is best. Stand about 3 feet from the wall and lean forward, placing your hands on the wall at about eye level. With your back straight and your heels firmly planted, press your upper body as close to the wall as you can and hold the position for a few seconds. Straighten your arms and push back to a standing position. Repeat the exercise 5 times.

When you're in competition, plan to finish your warm-up exercises about 15 minutes before your event is scheduled to begin. In a sense, warming up, means just that. Your exercises should bring your body temperature to the level required for the event. When you're finished exercising, don clothing that will keep your body temperature at the level you've attained.

In those final minutes before the race begins, try to perform some ritual that will help you to relax. Maybe it's just sitting calmly by yourself, visualizing what you plan to do, your strategy and form.

The excitement you feel before a race has practical value. A chemical called adrenalin, produced by the adrenal glands, speeds up your pulse rate and prepares the blood vessels so they can handle the body's increasing oxygen flow.

When your event is over, you should spend almost as much time warming down as you did warming up. You have to relax your muscles. Fail to do so, and they're likely to be sore the next day. Jogging is the best way to warm down. Don your sweats and lightly jog at least 2 laps — a half a mile.

2

Sprinting

While the classic idea of the sprinter is that of a tall and sleek athlete, the truth is that sprinters come in all shapes and sizes. The best evidence of this is probably Bob Hayes, who held the world record in the 100-yard dash before Ivory Crockett and Houston McTear came along (McTear and Crockett lowered the record to 9 seconds; Hayes' best was 9.1).

Hayes was built like a weight lifter. He had a starting style that made coaches wince. Seldom was he out of the blocks first. He ran pigeon toed. His body swayed from side to side as he charged toward the finish. Yet he still managed to win acclaim as the "world's fastest human." What Hayes did was compensate, developing a running style that enabled him to get the very most of his well-muscled body.

A sprinter can be short and squat, or tall and lean. It doesn't matter. What does matter is that you have the strength of body to handle your height and weight. Sprinting is an explosive feat that requires a maximum amount of effort over a short span of time. For this you need superior muscle reaction and speed, and overall body co-ordination.

If you watch twelve different sprinters, you're likely to see as many as a dozen different sprinting styles, but all of the runners will have at least one trait in common: They will all run on their toes (which is why track shoes that sprinters wear have spikes only on the front half of the sole). When you run on your toes, you thrust off from the forward part of your foot on each stride, and this not only tends to project you forward, but it helps to give you a longer stride. And longer strides are more efficient strides, getting you around the track faster.

Running on your toes also encourages you to lean forward as you run. When you lean forward, you're letting gravity help you. Keep your body erect and you lose this benefit. Not only will your speed be slowed, but you'll get fatigued faster.

High knee action is also important. This is something to cultivate in every sprint race, no matter the distance. When you lift the knee high, you're able to swing your lower leg

Houston McTear—"In short sprints, it's all in the start.

Houston McTear
Muhammad Ali Track Club

World Indoor Record, 60-yard dash, 1978 (6.05)
AAU Champion, 60-yard dash, 1978

In the short sprints, it's all in the start. That's where the race is won or lost. A young runner should spend as much as 60 per cent of his time working on his start and the first three or four steps. After those first three or four steps, you just relax, run your race. The start is the thing. If you don't get it at the start, you don't get it at the end.

forward farther, increasing the length of your stride.

If lifting your knees high when you run doesn't feel natural to you, there are a couple of drills that you can do to help you gain facility. Jog along at a leisurely pace, then break into a fast run, but with exaggerated knee action, lifting each knee in turn to above hip level. The burst of speed can last 10 to 20 seconds. Don't be concerned about covering a great amount of ground. In fact, you may only cover a few yards. You're only aim should be to get your knees pumping in pistonlike fashion. Jog a short distance, then repeat the exercise. Another drill is to run in place, holding your hands out in front of your body at waist level. As you pump your legs, bring your knees up to touch your palms.

When you are doing knee-lift exercises, or any other sprint drill, you should also concentrate on what you're doing with your arms. The faster you swing your arms, the faster your legs will move.

Keep the elbows at about a 90-degree angle. The hands should move forward and back, tracing an arc that brings them no higher than the shoulder on their forward swing, and to about hip level as they swing back. What you don't want to do is swing your hands across the front of your body. Keeping your elbows close to your sides will help to prevent this.

If you're inclined to be tense, be careful about making fists when you sprint. This is a mistake. Making a fist can cause tension in your arms and shoulders. It's just as bad to

Brenda Morehead — "You gotta hang in there."

Brenda Morehead
Tennessee State University

AAU Championship Record, 60-yard dash, 1978 (6.73)
AAU Champion, 60-yard dash, 1978, 1977

You gotta hang in there. It's hard sometimes, especially when you're young, in high school. That's when I had problems and thought about quitting. You don't know what's ahead. You don't realize the potential you have. You keep asking yourself, 'Is it really worth it?' But you gotta hang in there. You gotta have someone that believes in you and tells you not to quit. My family — I'm the seventh of ten children — helped me, backed me. My mother and father told me to keep working, keep trying. I owe them a lot.

run with your fingers stretched straight. Instead, cup your hands naturally as you run. Touching your middle finger to your thumb serves to encourage cupping.

Some coaches make much of body lean. Although you run in more of an upright position as you move into your normal sprinting stride, you're still not erect. What's important about body lean is that you don't merely lean forward from the waist; that's wrong. Your body leans forward in one piece; your back is perfectly straight. To get an idea of what this feels like, put your hands on a wall, keeping them at about the level of your head. Then back up as far as you can. Keep your chin up; look at your hands. Next, stand on your toes and raise one knee at a time. Notice how straight your back is. Also notice the amount of power you're generating with your big thigh muscles.

If you're a sprint specialist, the training program your coach sets down for you is certain to include interval running. This involves alternatively running and jogging over set distances. Interval training builds both speed and endurance.

Suppose the race in which you specialize is the 200 meters. Then two or three days a week you might be assigned to do a series of three or four 300-meter sprints with short periods of jogging in between.

On other days, you're likely to work on starts, on coming out of the blocks and running 30 or 40 yards each time. Sometimes sprinters are also assigned to do distance running to build their stamina.

THE SPRINT START

Your school will provide you with adjustable starting blocks. When setting the blocks, the first thing to decide is which foot to place back and which forward. A right-handed athlete usually makes the right foot the rear foot. Or you can try this: stand with your feet parallel and several inches apart. Lean forward from the waist. Keep leaning. Eventually you'll step forward with one foot to prevent yourself from falling. The foot you use to catch yourself should be your rear foot in the blocks.

Next, you have to determine the distance between the front and rear blocks. There are three different spacings: bunched, elongated, and medium. In the bunched position, the toe of the rear foot is opposite the heel of the front foot. Many coaches recommend this style because they feel it makes the runner more explosive than the other positions. But the bunched position can be uncomfortable for a runner who is taller than average.

When the blocks are in an elongated position, the knee of the rear leg is opposite the front foot. In the medium position, the midpoint of the rear calf is opposite the front foot.

Some coaches say that you get most power from the medium start, since the muscles of both legs work at their greatest effectiveness. But it's more a matter of individual preference than anything else. Experiment with the various settings until you determine the one that puts you at ease, but still permits you to burst forward with the utmost power.

The starter gives three commands: "Take your mark!" "Set!" and "Go!" On each, you assume a different body position.

When you hear, "Take your mark!" walk forward toward the starting line and stand in front of it. Then squat down so your hands are touching the track and pedal back, one foot at a time, placing your soles against the blocks. Adjust your back foot first, then your front foot. Press firmly.

Next, adjust your hands behind the standing line, spacing them about shoulder-width apart. The rules say that your hands cannot touch the line.

Your thumb and forefinger should form a line that you place parallel to the starting line. Spread your fingers so they'll be able to support your weight. Straighten your arms. Now your weight should be distributed evenly between your fingers and the knee of your rear leg.

You must be able to support the body's weight with the fingertips, at least in part. Doing so enables you to lean forward farther, and it's this forward lean that helps to assure

"Take your mark!" Pedal back into the blocks. Adjust your hands.

you'll get away fast. If you're a beginner, this position may feel uncomfortable, particularly if your fingers lack strength. But you can develop this strength by doing push-ups from your fingertips. Begin by doing 2 or 3 each day, trying to add to the number each week.

When you hear the command, "Set!" raise your hips and ease your weight forward. Your head should be beyond the starting line and your shoulders should be about even with it. Shift your weight far enough forward so you feel you're approaching the point of being off balance.

Your eyes should be on the track a few feet beyond the starting line. Be careful not to raise your chin too high. Doing so can cause you to straighten up as you come out of the

"Get set!" Raise your hips. Ease your weight forward.

blocks. You don't want to do that; you want to stay low.

One fault that young sprinters sometimes display is the inability to relax. As they raise up for the start, all they're thinking about is reaching the tape first. They clench their fists; they grit their teeth; they scowl. Such tension assures failure. Of course, you can't be casual about what you're going to be doing. You have to be in control; you have to concentrate. But if you clench your fists, grit your teeth, or scowl, it's a sign you're too tight. You must be relaxed.

In practice sessions, train yourself to hold your set position for slightly more than two seconds. Some runners try to time the raising of the upper body so that they're approaching the point of being off balance at the very instant the starter's pistol fires. This is called a rolling start, and it's illegal. You're not permitted to move from the time the command, "Set!" is issued until the gun goes off. If you do move, and an official sees the movement, a false start will be called. There's no penalty for one false start, but if you're guilty of two of them, you're disqualified. Starters, the rules declare, must "allow an interval of approximately two seconds, and when all are motionless, discharge the pistol."

Let's recap: You're in your set position, pushing hard against the blocks with your toes. Your weight is being carried by your toes and fingers. You're leaning forward, your hips slightly higher than your shoulders, approaching that off-balance point. Your eyes are focused on a point on the track a few yards beyond the starting line. Take a deep breath. Concentrate on the starter's pistol and what you're going to do when it fires.

At the crack of the pistol, your body reacts automatically, with every muscle working to get you into a full running stride as quickly as possible. You drive forward off your rear foot, with the arm on the other side ripping forward, too. Your movement must be outward, not upward.

You must be well balanced as you drive forward; you must be in control. This means that your strides have to be the right length, not too long or too short. It also means that

"Go!" Drive forward; pump your arms.

you have to pump your arms high. If you fail to bring your lead arm high on each stride, you won't be able to maintain your balance. You also won't be benefiting from the momentum that hard-pumping hands generate.

The first stride out of the blocks is the shortest. The second stride is an inch or so longer, and then each succeeding stride is a little bit longer than the one that precedes it, until you reach your full stride length.

Chandra Cheeseborough
Tennessee State University

World Record, Women's 220-yard dash, 1979 (6.71)
AAU Champion, 220-yard dash, 1979

Coming out of the blocks and maintaining momentum — that's what is important in this event [60-yard dash].
Get your knees up.
Pump your arms.
Relax.

You'll cover some 15 or 20 yards before you begin to settle into your normal sprinter's stride. The transition from a low, hard-driving accelerating stride to the longer, more upright sprinter's stride, has to be performed smoothly and effortlessly. The transition should be practically imperceptible to any onlooker.

No two starters are exactly alike in the way they start a race. Try to find out whatever you can about the starter assigned to your event. Is he a "fast gun"? Or does he give the runners time to settle into their blocks after instructing them to take their marks? Be prepared to adjust your time accordingly.

It's also a good idea to inspect the track before the race. Walk the entire oval. In the case of an outdoor track, look for holes. With an indoor track, look for high boards where one section abuts another.

If you have a chance to practice on the track before the race, do so by all means. Many runners take as many as from five to ten practice starts. If there is no opportunity to set up your blocks at the starting line and practice, then practice in the infield area.

The 200-meter and 220-yard sprints begin on a turn in the track, and the starting positions are staggered so as to compensate for the unequal distances competitors are to run. Runners in the outside lanes start ahead of those in the inside lanes.

In staggered starts, it's standard procedure to place one's blocks on the outside edges of the lane. This ensures your first few strides will be in a straight line (see illustration).

To sum up, the "secret" of a successful sprint start lies in these factors:

- A split-second reaction to the starter's pistol.
- Driving powerfully out of the blocks without raising to more of an upright position; that is, leaning while accelerating.
- Moving into your smooth running stride easily, naturally, without stumbling or wobbling.

One last piece of advice about starts — forget about your opponents. In your mind's eye, you should hold an image of what your body is going to be doing at the sound of the starter's pistol. And that's the only thing you should be thinking about. If you're thinking about the other runners, you'll never get away fast.

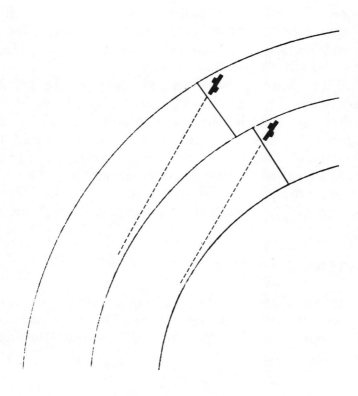

100 METERS; 110 YARDS

The 100-meter dash looks to be an all-out charge for the tape, and some instruction books describe it in those terms. But it's not quite as simple as that. It takes at least 5 or 6 seconds for a runner to reach top speed, in which time he covers 50 to 60 meters. It doesn't take long for the leg muscles to begin to tire — perhaps another 20 or 25 meters. What this means is that after 75 or 80 meters, the sprinter begins losing speed.

Your first ambition should be to get out of the blocks as fast as possible. Your second aim should be to do whatever you can to overcome the strain and fatigue you're going to feel in the late stages of the dashes. You've got to concentrate on keeping your stride going. Pump your knees hard; drive off from your toes. You're not trying to go any faster, remember. You reach your topmost speed at, say, 60 meters. All you're attempting to do is maintain that speed for as long as you can.

Some runners use special techniques at the finish line, throwing out their arms or leaping toward the tape. Be wary about such tactics. They can cause you to break stride, and thus do you more harm than good.

You'll be hearing about runners who use a dip finish. As the tape is neared, the runner begins to lean forward more, and in his last stride he thrusts both arms behind his body, which forces his shoulders and arms forward. It's said that a smartly executed dip finish can gain an advantage of one full inch over a rival who stays perfectly upright at the tape. But again there's the problem of disrupting your stride. The best policy is to simply concentrate on running through the tape.

200 METERS; 220 YARDS

If you're successful at 100 meters, it doesn't necessarily mean that you will be at 200 meters. There's an additional skill involved, the skill of "floating" or "coasting" through the middle stage of the race.

Always run through the tape.

To "float" means to run as fast as possible with as little effort as possible. Did you ever help a friend push a car to get it started? It takes enormous effort at the start to get the vehicle rolling. But once it's moving, you don't have to work so hard to keep in going. That's analogous to "floating."

From a standpoint of technique, divide the 200 meter dash into three parts: the start and acceleration to full speed; the float; and the final drive to the wire.

In its early stages the 200 is about the same as the 100. You explode away at the gun, extending every muscle in your body to reach full speed. You'll cover 50 to 60 meters during this phase. Then you float. This doesn't mean that you should ease up. You're still at full speed, but you're relaxed—at less than full effort. This may sound inconsistent, but once you try it you'll find that it's not hard to accomplish.

At a point some 40 to 50 meters from the finish line, gather yourself for the final spurt to the tape. Your body aches in a hundred places. But you must drive yourself harder, pulling your knees higher, pumping your arms more. Even if you manage to do this, accept the fact that your performance will be lower in these final stages.

The 200-meter and 220-yard dashes each involve one turn. Naturally, you're not going to be able to run the curve as fast as you run a straightaway, but you can keep from slowing down too much if you remember to pump your outside arm— your right arm—across your body as you're negotiating the curve. When you do this, you'll increase your inward lean, and this counteracts the detrimental effects of the centrifugal force your body generates as you speed around the turn. In other words, pumping the arm across the body can make turning easier. Also, run as close as possible to the inside of the lane. This reduces the distance around the turn.

As you come out of the turn, resume pumping your arms in the normal way. You're driving for the finish line at this point. If you've negotiated the turn without easing up, it will seem as if you're speeding up when you come out of the turn. This gives you an emotional boost at a time when you can use it to good advantage.

Frieda Nichols — "You've got to get out."

Freida Nichols
D.C. Striders

All-Comers Indoor Record, 220-yard dash, 1978 (24.23)

You've got to get out. That's the most important thing. Even though you're not in the blocks, you should treat the start like a 60-yard start, and get away fast.

The last 60 yards are important, too. You've got to be in control. You've got to keep your speed going. Use your arms. Once you've got your arms pumping, your knees will come up and keep your speed up.

Tommie Smith of the United States, who established the world record at 200 meters—19.83 seconds—in 1968, and held it throughout the 1970s, could run the turn at almost full speed. But what was really devastating to his opponents was the way he came off the turn shooting ahead, actually accelerating in the final yards to the tape.

When you compete in a race such as the 200-meter dash, or whenever you try to go all out for as long as you can, you're certain to feel pain, not the kind of pain that is caused by injury, but real pain, nevertheless—the pain that an athlete experiences as the point of exhaustion draws closer and closer. It might start in the legs or thighs and work up into your back and shoulders. Your lungs seem as if they are going to burst. Your throat burns.

How you deal with this pain is important. You know that if you slow down or quit the pain will quickly diminish. But you can't let yourself quit. You have to have the courage to push yourself through the pain barrier. Try to forget about the pain. Instead, think about all of the hours you've put into training and practice. Think about how your hard work will be wasted—if you quit. Think about pleasant things, about the big ice cream cone you're going to buy yourself when the race is over. Think about your girlfriend or your boyfriend.

Again, I'm not talking about the kind of pain that is related to injury, only about the pain brought on by fatigue. As one runner told me, "I don't feel I've had a good workout unless I've experienced pain."

3

Hurdling

In hurdling, the idea is to spring over the hurdles, not jump over them. This means to excel you have to be tall and sleek. Most hurdlers are about 6 feet in height by the time they reach college. You don't have to be a 6-footer to be a high school hurdler, but there's no disputing the fact that the longer your legs, the better you're going to do.

What's said above applies no matter the type of hurdling event, which covers quite a range, varying in hurdle height, the space between hurdles, and the length of the event. The chief differences are between low hurdles and high hurdles. The low hurdles are 30 inches in height. In high school competition, the high hurdles are 33 inches for women, 39 inches for men. College hurdlers must leap over 42-inch hurdles.

In high school competition, indoor hurdling events can be 50 or 80 yards. Outdoor hurdling events can be as long as 400 meters.

If you're wholly inexperienced at hurdling, there's a drill that will give you the feel of what it's like. It's a walking drill. Set three hurdles at the 30-inch height and place them on a track, spacing them 10 yards apart. Walk toward the first hurdle as if you were going to pass it a few inches to the left or right (to the left, if your lead leg is going to be your left leg; to the right, if you are going to lead with your right leg). Plant your lead foot a few inches behind the hurdle. Lean forward, shifting your weight to the lead foot, and snap the trailing foot over the hurdle.

Notice that when you lean forward, your trailing leg comes forward to clear the hurdle easily and naturally. Of course, you have to turn your trailing foot outward so it won't strike the barrier. Walk through the three-hurdle course several times, establishing the feeling of what it's like to plant the lead foot beyond the hurdle and pull the trailing foot over.

The next phase is to perform the drill while jogging. But when you jog over the course, change your technique a bit. Instead of merely planting the lead foot, take an "air step" with it. Lift the lead foot to about half the height of the hurdle. Lean forward. Again, you'll notice how you're trailing leg snaps smartly over the barrier.

Now you're ready to try a "real" hurdling drill. Line up squarely in front of a low hurdle, and approach it at about half speed, throw your lead leg over, lean forward, then snap the trailing leg over. Keep running in stride.

By this time, you may have noticed that your arm action

Deby LaPlante
San Diego State University

U.S. Indoor Record, Women's 60-yard hurdles, 1978 (7.53)
AAU Champion, Women's 60-yard hurdles, 1978

Before you try this event competitively, be sure to learn a technique. That way you don't develop a lot of bad habits — as I did. I've been competing for ten years and I still have some of them.

Once you begin competing, try to get involved in the Junior Olympics. It's a good program. If you're at all decent, you have a good chance of winning. That's important. It gives you confidence. I entered the Junior Olympics when I was fourteen and I won. I won again at seventeen. It helped me a lot.

Deby LaPlante (right)—"Before you try [hurdling], be sure to learn a technique."

is almost as important as what you're doing with your legs. It's your arms that help to keep your body square to the hurdles and evenly balanced as you go over each barrier.

If your right leg is your lead leg as you go over, then it should be your left arm that is reaching out. This increases your momentum. It helps you in leaning, too. As for your right arm, keep it close to your body.

What's really critical is your lead-leg technique. You must drive the knee of that leg up, lifting it hard and high. The knee itself is slightly bent. You have to be aggressive, pushing off with as much force as you can possibly muster. You must think in terms of bursting over the barrier, not merely sailing over it.

Continue to push off with the trailing foot until the trailing leg is fully extended. At the same time, you're lowering your head, almost as if you're driving forward from the waist.

As the knee of your lead leg gets to the level of your chest, the sole of the foot—not the toes—should be aimed straight ahead. The knee is still slightly bent.

Your lead leg should reach its greatest height, not at the moment you actually clear the barrier, but before you clear it. Some coaches tell their hurdlers the lead leg should be at its greatest height when at a point about 6 inches in front of the

---

Lacey O'Neal
President's Council on Physical Fitness

World Record Holder, 70-Yard Hurdles
U. S. Olympic Team, 1960

I'm controversial because I say this, but I think hurdling is simple. Hurdling is merely running over obstacles, nothing more. Concentrate on your sprinting. Don't worry about your hurdling technique, how your lead foot is positioned, whether you're holding your toes properly, and things like that. Think about running. You'll be more relaxed. People try to make hurdling complicated. I don't feel that it is.

Drive the knee of lead leg high.

hurdle. This technique enables you to go over with your lead leg slightly bent. It also helps to cushion your landing, so that you can drive off fast into the next stride. And, since you're actually driving *down* as you're lead leg goes over, you can pull your trailing leg over faster.

Get a friend to watch your form. Have him kneel so his eyes will be level with the top of the hurdle as you go over it. He'll then be able to tell whether you're reaching your greatest height 6 inches in front of the hurdle. You should be about 4 inches above the top level of the hurdle at that point.

As the toes of the lead leg reach the ground and the trailing leg comes forward, it's important to keep the trailing

As you go over, the sole of the lead foot should lead the way.

leg high, ready for the next stride. You must land with your shoulders square. Otherwise, you won't forge straight ahead. Any deviation to the right or left costs you precious time, of course.

Incidentally, if you hit a hurdle as you attempt to go over it, there's no penalty. Even if you knock one over, you haven't violated any rule. But hitting a hurdle slows you down or can cause you to make a damaging adjustment in your form.

Rod Milburn, who dominated hurdling in the early 1970s and captured the gold medal for the United States at Munich in 1972, won with his speed. Willie Davenport, the 1968 Olympic gold medalist, depended more on his graceful form.

But Renaldo ("Skeets") Nehemiah, who established himself as the best hurdler in the world during the late 1970s, had the speed of Milburn and the finesse of Davenport. In addition, Nehemiah had power, with tremendous strength in his chest and arms. "Almost every hurdler depends strictly on his legs," Nehemiah once observed, "But I use my whole body to push me through, not just a portion of it." Indeed, sometimes Nehemiah seemed to be attacking the hurdles, rather than accepting them and merely sprinting over them in accepted fashion.

Keep the trailing leg high as you clear the bar, readying it for the next stride.

Renaldo ("Skeets") Nehemiah (right, with Charles Foster)
—"First, learn the event."

Renaldo Nehemiah
University of Maryland

World Record, 60-yard hurdles, 1978 (6.89)
World Record, 110-meter hurdles, 1979 (13.16)
AAU Champion, 60-yard hurdles, 1979

You really have to *want* to be a hurdler to be successful. You have to work at it. The first thing to do is learn the event. Watch every race you can. Watch different hurdlers and their styles. Pick up as many tips as you can. Try different things yourself. Talk to coaches. Ask questions. Go to clinics. There are all kinds of opportunities to help you learn and develop.

Nehemiah first started being noticed in 1977, when, as a high school senior, he was invited to participate in the Millrose Games, thus gaining recognition as potential world-class material. Although he was eliminated in the trial heats of the 60-yard high hurdles, he equalled the national high school record for the event.

Following the Millrose Games, Nehemiah went on to equal the high school indoor record six more times. He was even more impressive during the outdoor season. He twice equalled the high school hurdle record of 13.2 seconds, which had been set by Rod Milburn in 1969, three years before his victory at Munich. Then, competing in the Eastern High School Championships, Nehemiah broke the record by three-tenths of a second with a spectacular clocking of 12.9 seconds. He followed this with a victory in the American junior championships and another win while representing the United States against the Soviet Union. In the last-named meet, he registered 13.5 seconds over the international high hurdles, cutting two-tenths of a second off of another scholastic mark.

As this suggests, Nehemiah's competitive instincts are strong. He was a quarterback at Fanwood High School in Scotch Plains, New Jersey, before he started winning headlines in the hurdles.

He comes from a close-knit family. "We do a lot together," a younger sister, Lisa, once said. "If one of us is participating in sports activities or anything, we all go to watch. We take trips together. We go to church together." In the years that "Skeets" was growing up, his father took a second job at a gas station to help make ends meet.

Nehemiah credits much of his success to his start. As a young teen-ager in Scotch Plains, where he became the only high schooler in history to break 13 seconds for either 120 yards or 110 meters, Nehemiah used to practice starts in his room, hurdling over his bed. He put full-length mirrors on the wall so he could inspect his form.

A coach, Dick Hill, gave an important tip. "He told me

to come out looking straight at the first hurdle," Nehemiah once recalled. "I had a habit of driving with my head down."

The transition from high school (39 inch) hurdles to the standard (42 inch) barriers can be troublesome for an athlete. Not for Nehemiah. Not only had he competed over the taller hurdles at the end of his high school career, but he had practiced over them regularly. "We felt that the high school hurdles were too low for him," Jean Poquette, Nehemiah's high school coach, once said. "He was able to get over them so easily that we were afraid he would make mistakes in technique if there were no challenge. To avoid forming bad habits, he trained on 42-inch and sometimes even 45-inch hurdles."

As a University of Maryland freshman, Nehemiah returned to the Millrose Games to win at 60 yards, setting a world indoor record of 7.07 seconds. He did even better than that in the 55-meter high hurdles at the U. S. Olympic Invitational meet at Madison Square Garden in January 1979, establishing a world record with the spectacular time of 6.88 seconds. The 55-meter distance is 5.35 inches longer than 60 yards.

That night, Russ Rogers, the coach at Essex County (New Jersey) College and a former world-class hurdler, timed Nehemiah's start, and determined that he had reached the first hurdle in 1.7 seconds. "That's almost impossible," said Rogers. "I don't know of anyone that has ever gone faster than 1.9 seconds."

The official program for the Millrose Games in 1979 declared: "Tonight, Nehemiah will successfully defend his Millrose title and perhaps lower his record again. Later this year, he will break the world outdoor record in the 110-meter highs, and in 1980 he will win that event in the Olympic Games in Moscow."

That night, Nehemiah did successfully defend his Millrose title. He missed the world record by one one-hundredth of a second, because, as some observers noted, he slowed to raise the forefinger in a No. 1 signal as he crossed the finish line. By the time the indoor season ended, Nehemiah had set records at 50 and 60 yards and at 50 and 55 meters.

Ever since his high school days, Nehemiah has been compared to Rod Milburn, who represented Southern University. In the year following his Olympic championship of 1972, Milburn joined the professional track tour, and retired — unwillingly — in 1975 after the enterprise folded. In winning the Olympic crown, Milburn defeated the 1968 gold medalist. He was the first man ever to run the 120-yard high hurdles in 13 seconds flat. (Automatic timing, now required in hurdles, yields times that are about .25 seconds slower than hand timing in the 120-yard hurdles.) Milburn once held the 110-meter high hurdles record of 13.24 seconds.

"It's an honor to be compared to Milburn," Nehemiah said in 1978. "He has been my idol. I want to succeed him. But as far as the world record is concerned, I'm not going to make an obsession of it. It will come one day."

No one doubted that. Neil Amdur, who covered track and field for the New York *Times,* was quoted as saying, "I'm convinced that by 1980 he'll break 13 seconds." Frank Costello, Nehemiah's coach, agreed, saying that he was "capable of doing it."

At the AAU Indoor Track and Field Championships at Madison Square Garden in February 1979, just a few minutes before the women's hurdles were run, Nehemiah introduced himself to one of the entrants, and offered her a pointer on how to get more speed coming over a hurdle. The contestant's name was Canzetta ("Candy") Young, a sixteen-year-old junior at Beaver Falls, Pennsylvania, High School. After the conversation with Nehemiah, Candy Young went out and won the 60-yard hurdles with a world record of 7.50 seconds, beating Deby LaPlante, who held the former record of 7.53 seconds, in the process. Candy was later voted the best woman athlete of the meet.

Candy's high school coach, Karlin Ryan, admitted that his knowledge of hurdling was less than profound, and that he was learning hurdling right along with his prize pupil. Up until her AAU victory, Candy's only real instruction in hurdling's fine points came during a one-week session at the U. S. Olympic training camp at Colorado Springs in the summer of 1978.

Beaver Falls High is less than ideal as a training facility. When Beaver Valley was under snow, Candy had to practice in one of the high school's hallways, one just long enough to set up three hurdles. In the spring, when she finally got a chance to face a standard 10-hurdle set-up again, it looked like a marathon course to her.

THE START

As in any sprint, the hurdling start is decisive. As the starter's pistol fires, drive hard out of the blocks, just as if it were a 60-yard sprint. But try to get your hips higher. When you reach that first hurdle, you want to have your center of gravity high enough so you can simply skim over it, not jump over it.

Once you've determined which leg is going to be your starting leg, plan the number of strides you're going to take in your approach. In the 100-yard and 110-meter hurdles, most athletes take eight strides from the starting blocks to the first

In short races, hurdling start is just like a sprint start.

hurdle. If you're particularly long-legged, you might use only seven.

Work out the number of approach steps through a trial and error process. If you find eight steps to be right for you, but you're hitting your take-off spot with the "wrong" foot, that is, with your lead foot instead of your take-off foot, that's no problem. Simply reverse the position of your feet in the starting blocks.

As you leave the blocks, concentrate on the top of the first hurdle. Carry your arms high and start moving your shoulders forward so you will be able to lean easily when you reach your take-off point.

LOW HURDLES

Your stride should be simply a long sprint stride when you compete in the low hurdles. And your forward body lean doesn't have to be as great as a high hurdler's. It doesn't have to be much more than the lean you use when sprinting.

If you're particularly tall, be sure you're not going too high over the hurdles. This costs you seconds. If you are soaring too high, it may be because you're taking off too close to the hurdle. You're leaping up, not stretching forward.

In the 100-meter and 110-yard hurdles, you have to go over 10 hurdles. Take 3 strides between hurdles. Quickness of leg action is very important. There's no need to pump your knees high, but use plenty of arm action.

What was said in the previous chapter about the finish of a sprint race applies here. Once you've cleared the last hurdle, make every effort to sprint the tape. But don't make the mistake of trying to sprint too soon. Wait until your trailing leg is beginning to swing forward. Young hurdlers, in their frantic effort to get to the finish line after driving over the last hurdle, sometimes start to sprint — or, at least, attempt to sprint — before their feet have touched the ground. This disrupts their stride; it can mean the difference between first place and finishing out of the money.

In the low hurdles, use a long sprinter's stride in going over.

HIGH HURDLES

More preparation goes into clearing hurdles that are 33 inches or 39 inches in height. As soon as you go over one, you must start getting ready to go over the next one. Start moving your shoulders forward, so by the time you reach the hurdle you'll be leaning toward it. Get your lead leg up; you should feel like you're attacking the hurdle. The lead arm goes out to the side to help you maintain your balance. Your chest and shoulders are forward.

Once the trail leg is off the track, pull the knee up level with your hips. Your thigh should be about parallel with the ground as you go clear the crossbar.

High school boys compete in the 330-yard intermediate hurdles, sprinting all-out for 330 yards and clear 8 hurdles while doing it. This is one of the most demanding of all track events.

Again, take plenty of time to plan your steps. Most intermediate hurdlers use 15 steps between as many hurdles as they can. Fatigue may begin to set in after the fifth hurdle, whereupon you'll have to switch changeover to 17 steps between hurdles. If you need more than 17 steps, this isn't an event you should try; your times won't be fast enough.

Charles Foster
Philadelphia Pioneer Track Club

AAU Championship Record, 60-yard Hurdles, 1978 (7.11)
AAU Champion, 1978, 1975

Work hard.
Be dedicated.
That's all.

4

Middle-Distance Races

In high school track and field, races at 400 meters (440 yards) and 800 meters (880 yards or ½ mile) are considered middle-distance races. Speed is still vital at these distances, but a second factor looms. The longer the race, the more important it becomes. It's stamina.

If you plan to run in middle-distance or distance races, you must discipline and train your body toward achieving a state of oxygen balance. In this, the heart and bloodstream deliver and keep delivering sufficient oxygen to keep pace with your increased muscular activity. That's what stamina is all about.

Let's back up a bit. Every activity, from snapping your fingers to running a marathon, requires energy. The body produces energy by burning food. The agent that does the burning is oxygen.

But the problem is that the body can't store oxygen. We breath it in every moment of our lives. If the supply gets cut off, the amount of oxygen you have stored never lasts more than a few minutes. The brain and heart stop functioning.

The key to successful distance running is to get sufficient oxygen to all areas of the body where food is stored, so that the oxygen can combine with the food to produce energy. The capability of delivering oxygen varies from runner to runner. Imagine you're in a footrace with a friend, each of you to cover a half a mile. Over the first 100 yards or so, the two of you stay shoulder to shoulder. But then your friend starts dropping back. You keep increasing your lead. By the time you cross the finish line, you're 20 yards ahead. If you asked him why he didn't keep pace, he might say simply, "I got tired." In metabolic terms, what happened was that his body was unable to supply all the oxygen his energy output demanded.

To be a successful distance runner, you have to keep improving your body's ability to bring in and deliver oxygen to the cells where it combines with food to increase energy. You do this by improving the efficiency of your lungs, so they can process more air with less effort and by increasing the strength of your heart. A strong heart pumps more blood with fewer strokes. Do these two things and you'll increase your oxygen consumption. In other words, you'll build your stamina.

Interval training is one way to improve the strength of one's heart and lungs. When you embark on a program of in-

In middle-distance races, emphasis is on both speed and stamina.

terval training, you run a designated distance—110 yards, 220 yards, or 440 yards—and immediately follow the run with a recovery period of jogging or fast walking. Then the run is repeated and the recovery period is repeated. You and your coach decide how many repetitions you should do.

During the period you run, you create an oxygen debt. Your pulse rate zooms. During the period you jog or walk, the recovery period, your pulse rate drops. Such drills strengthen the heart and lungs, increasing the amount of blood pumped with each heartbeat, and this increases the amount of oxygen the body takes in.

One standard interval workout calls for a runner to run 220-yard dashes, allowing 32 to 35 seconds for each, with a 110-yard jog between each pair of dashes. The recovery period should be 90 seconds. Of course, you shouldn't attempt such a drill without your coach's approval.

As another means of building their stamina, middle-distance and distance runners often take part in fartlek running. "Fartlek" is a Swedish word meaning "speed play." A system made popular by Gosta Homer, one-time Swedish Olympic coach, fartlek running is a natural, informal way to train. "You run the way you feel," is the way it is often described.

Fartlek running is frequently done over a cross-country course. It can also be done at the beach, on a golf course, over bridle paths, or country roads—anyplace as long as you're away from the track.

Continuous movement is one of the chief characteristics of fartlek training. It doesn't matter whether the course you plan to cover is one mile or ten miles; you never once stop.

Variety is another characteristic. You're constantly switching from one form of movement to another, which is one reason that runners with low boring points enjoy this form of training. You might begin with a 5- to 10-minute period of easy running, this followed by some fast running for a half a mile. A period of jogging can come next. Then some sprints, short ones, 50 to 60 yards long, until you begin to feel tired. You can then go back to jogging or maybe some fast walking.

You tailor the fartlek program to your capabilities and the events in which you specialize. At most, the distance should be about 10 miles, and the time involved, two hours. It shouldn't be a long, slow run, but, on the other hand, it shouldn't leave you so fatigued that you have to drag yourself home. Strike a happy medium. Most of all, plan a program that you're going to enjoy. Enjoyment is the essential ingredient of fartlek training.

The best middle-distance runner of recent times is Cuba's Alberto Juantorena, who, at Montreal, became the first in Olympic history to win both the 400 meters and 800 meters. Jim Bush, track coach at UCLA, called Juantorena's double win "the greatest feat in Olympic history." John Walker of New Zealand, winner of the gold medal in the 1,500 meters, hailed the Cuban as "the athlete of tomorrow."

Up until 1976, Juantorena was known as a very fine 400-meter runner. Period. But his ability to sustain his speed over the entire 400-meter distance, not struggle over the last 50 meters as most runners do, impressed his coach, and he began having Juantorena try some distance work in 1975. "When he told me he was thinking about the 800, I thought he was crazy," Juantorena once recalled. But when his training times kept improving, Juantorena began to buy the idea.

In the Olympics, the 800 meters was on the program first. Observers believed that Juantorena's strategy would be to lay back, hoping that the front runners would misjudge the pace, and then use his sprinter's speed to overtake them at the end. But Juantorena had other plans. As the bunched runners came out of the first turn and into the backstretch, Juantorena eased into the lead. Rick Wohlhuter of the United States, the favorite and world record holder at the distance, took over second place, not far behind.

As the field barrelled through the front stretch the first time, Juantorena clung to the lead, maintaining his sprinter's stride. The experts waited for him to fade. Into the final turn Juantorena pounded. Now Wohlhuter began to close the gap, but Juantorena never faltered. In the stretch, Wohlhuter's face twisted into a scowl and Juantorena pulled away from him. Not only did he win, but he did so in world-record time, 1:43.5.

The question remained whether the victory had taken too much out of Juantorena for the 400 meters. The answer came 100 meters from the finish when Juantorena surged past Fred Newhouse of the United States. The Cuban was almost two full strides ahead at the tape.

Juantorena does not look like what a sprinter is supposed to look like. He is 6 feet, 3 inches and weighs 185. (At Montreal, someone remarked that Rich Wohlhuter, who is of conventional sprinter size, looked like Juantorena's younger brother.) He runs with awesomely long strides. To win, he just goes out and overpowers every challenger.

400 METERS; 440 YARDS (¼ MILE)

To track enthusiasts, the 440-yard dash — the quarter mile — has a special excitement. This distance is just about as far as an athlete can push himself at top speed. In outdoor competition, the 440 is run once around the track. But indoors, with an oval with 10, 11, or 12 laps to the mile, 440 yards is an awkward distance because the start or finish is likely to fall close to a curve. Thus, indoor meets often represent races at distances of 500 yards or 600 yards.

From the standpoint of technique, the 400-meter race is somewhat similar to the 200-meter dash. It requires a fast start, the ability to accelerate quickly, a float, and a drive.

But your form should be different than a sprinter's form. While you should pump your knees high as a sprinter does, you should land more on the balls of your feet as you stride, rather than on the toes.

Your stride should be shorter than a sprinter's stride.

Madison Square Garden—11 laps to the mile.

And there's less forward lean than in sprinting. Swing your arms forward and back, keeping them close to your body. But there's no need to swing them vigorously. Carry them low; keep them relaxed.

Of course, when you're cutting to the pole, attempting to pass, or seeking to prevent an opponent from passing, and you have to shift into high gear, you'll have to use more of a sprinter's stride. Once you've achieved your tactical goal, resume using your middle-distance form.

When it comes to tactics, there's some controversy. Up until the 1960s, sprinters always ran the 400 meter dash just as they did the 200 meter—going all out in the initial stages. Then along came Lee Evans, gold medalist in the 1968 Olympics, and the world record holder (43.86 seconds). Evans finished at a blistering pace, actually running the first half and

In middle distance running, you're more erect when you stride. Keep your arms low, relaxed.

last half of the race in the same time. His opponents, all of whom expended their greatest efforts in the early stages of the race, were no match for him at the end.

But running the 400-meter dash with a finishing kick is no easy matter. Consider Lee Evans to be a miracle man. The 400 meter is, after all, a sprint, and if you try to save something for the end, it's almost certain you'll be too far behind to catch up.

The more usual way to run the race is to burst out of the blocks as if you were running the 100-yard dash. Accelerate until you attain your upright sprinter's stride. As you enter the first turn, keep to the inside of your lane and pump your

Kim Thomas—"You've got to train hard, if you want to win."

Kim Thomas
Police Athletic League, New York City

U.S. Indoor Record, Women's 440-yard run, 1978 (55.53)
National AAU Champion, Women's 440-yard run, 1978

This is a tough event. It's sprint all the way. I train four days a week, two hours every session. You've got to train hard if you want to be good.

right arm across your body, which encourages you to lean into the turn. Keep up the pace as you pound out of the turn. Now start floating, running relaxed while holding your speed.

The final curve is where many runners lose the race, because they slow down without knowing they are doing so. Be aggressive as you enter the curve, pumping your outside arm across your body. Maintain your speed. Keep your legs pumping high.

If you run the final turn well, you'll come into the final straightaway with the feeling you're accelerating. To *actually* accelerate at this point is a formidable task. Fatigue is closing in. You need tremendous courage just to maintain your speed. But the key element is that final turn. If you can float through that turn without losing speed, the final yards to the wire will not be a problem.

A staggered start is used in running the 400 meter and 440-yard races, which means that the inside lane is the choice lane. If you're in the inside lane, the other runners will be strewn out ahead of you, and you'll be able to keep an eye on them as you run. But don't turn this into a disadvantage by trying to make up the stagger too soon. You have to run your own race. Don't let yourself be influenced by what the opposition is doing.

Stan Vinson
University of Chicago Track Club
AAU Champion, 600-yard run, 1979, 1978

Even more than the 800, the 600 is a thinking man's race. You're never out of the running as long as you don't let yourself get boxed in.

Uncertainty can be your worst enemy. Never be afraid to make a move. Once you've made your move and gotten position, you go from there.

In races with a staggered start, the inside lane is considered the choice lane.
The runner there can keep an eye on his rivals.

800 METERS; 880 YARDS
($\frac{1}{2}$ MILE)

In races that are 800 meters or longer, only two commands are given by the starter—"Take your mark!" and "Go!" Instead of a crouch, a standing start is used. One foot is placed ahead of the other, the toes at the starting line. You lean forward, putting your weight on the front foot. When the pistol fires, drive off the back foot and swing the arm opposite forward. If your left foot is the rear foot, push off from that foot and swing your right arm forward. This technique gets you off to a fast start and keeps your body square.

Either a staggered start or a scratch start may be used in the 800 meters. In a scratch start, the runners line up straight across the track, that is, there's no adjusting the runner's starting points to compensate for the unequal distances involved.

The rules governing a staggered start say that runners must stay in their assigned lanes during the sprint down the straightway, until reaching the first turn. Then you're permitted to "cut to the pole," that is, move to the inside. In the case of a scratch start, you cut to the inside as soon as you want after the firing of the gun.

You do have to exercise some caution, however. The rules state you must be at least two running strides ahead of the runner you're cutting in front of before you make your move. The purpose of this rule is to prevent accidents. If you tried to cut in front of a runner who was matching you almost stride for stride, a collision would be a certainty.

Strategy is crucial. Before the start, you should decide how you're going to run the race. You can shoot into the lead at the beginning and attempt to stay there throughout the race. Other front runners prefer a different technique. Rather than get caught up in a scramble for the lead in the first 100 meters, they elect to wait until around the 200-meter mark before attempting to move ahead of the pack. They then try to stay there until they reach the tape. Another alternative is

"Take your mark!" "Go!" Drive off from your rear foot and pump the arm opposite forward.

to run at a steady, comfortable pace, saving some energy for a finishing burst.

Whichever strategy you decide upon, you must know the pace at which the race is being run. If the pace is too fast, it's better to drop off slightly, no matter what your strategy might be, and let other runners open up a lead, rather than try to run beyond your capability. In the last 50 or 60 meters of the 800, the pace invariably slows. And the runner who has read the pace the best, and adjusted his speed accordingly, is able to make up considerable distance.

After getting off to a good start, it's usually wise to settle down somewhere near the tail end of the field. Then what you do depends on the other runners. If the field moves efficiently but not with stunning speed, wait until the final lap before making your move.

But if the leaders set a bristling pace and the field begins to string out, make your move sooner. Don't rush, however. Improve your position slowly, steadily.

In order to be able to do any of the strategic planning recommended in the preceding paragraphs, you must be able to judge the pace of the field and, at the same time, measure your own speed and endurance. This takes practice. You're not entirely on your own, however. At the halfway mark—at 400 meters of the 800 meter race—an official will call out the elapsed time. You should get a friend to stand at or near the 200-meter mark and call out your time to you when you pass that point.

The most decisive moments in the 800 meter race occur in the final back straight, when you're 200 to 300 meters from the finish. It's then that you must improve your position so that you will be poised for that final burst to the tape. This means you can't allow yourself to be boxed in as you enter the final straight; you have to be free to launch your thrust. This is another reason why it's smart to remain off the pace in this event. It's better to be slotted fifth or sixth and have a clear track ahead than be wedged in behind the leader as the race comes down to its final stages.

5

Distance Running

Everything you do as a distance runner has to be done with the idea of conserving as much energy as possible. You have to run economically.

Your stride must be a short one, even shorter than the stride used by a middle-distance runner. Because your stride is short, you don't require much knee action.

Each stride involves a ball-heel-ball action. You land on the ball of your foot, roll back onto the heel, then rock forward onto the ball again to push off with the toes. This is opposed to the sprinter's stride. A sprinter lands on his toes. If you tried to run on your toes for a distance event, your calf muscles would develop painful cramps. It might be only a quarter of a mile before this began to happen.

You also must carry your upper body more erect when you run distance events. This helps to give more freedom to your hips, which enables you to get more rhythm into your strides. If there is one characteristic that sets a distance runner apart from a sprinter, it is his rhythmic, relaxed manner of running. Sometimes this is a natural gift, but it is usually developed through long, dedicated training sessions.

Wilson Waigwa — "Start easy. Be comfortable. Don't push yourself."

Wilson Waigwa
Philadelphia Pioneer Track Club
World-Class Miler (3.53:2, 1978)

A beginner [in the 1,500 meters or mile] should work on building his stamina first, and not worry about speed. Start easy. Run a mile a day for a week. Run two miles a day the next week. But be comfortable. Take it easy. Don't push yourself. Each week increase your distance by another mile. But keep taking it easy. You're not in a race. At the end of six weeks, you should be running as many as six miles a day. Then you should see a coach. What happens next is up to him.

How you carry your arms is pretty much a matter of personal preference. Keep them relaxed; let them swing easily. Cup your fingers so as to prevent your forearms from tensing up.

Breathe as naturally as you can. Keep your mouth open so you can draw as much oxygen as possible into your lungs each time you inhale.

On entering a curve, runners are in single file in the inside lane. Stay as close to the inside of the lane as you can. Lean into the curve and pump your right arm more vigorously. When you come out of the curve and into the straightaway, go back to using your normal standard technique.

In a distance race, passing is sometimes difficult. The field runs in single file, everyone clinging to the inside of the inside lane. To get by someone, you have to pull to the outside and turn on added speed, then ease back to the inside. In other words, you have to go faster than your rival while covering more ground.

It can happen that you'll get lucky. As you're rounding a curve, the runner just ahead of you might swing a bit wide, and you'll get an opening on the inside. You can zip through, passing him without too much extra effort. But this is a rare occurrence. In virtually every case, you'll have to go to the outside.

It's best to do your passing on a straightaway; on curves, you have to cover extra added distance. The advantage you have when passing is that you can take your opponent by surprise. So when you do decide to make your move, don't give any warning you're coming. Move decisively. Begin by picking up your speed and getting as close to your opponent as you can, then swing to the outside, using your increased momentum to carry you right by the rival. Really turn on the speed at this point. You don't want him to be able to answer your challenge by speeding up. If he does that, it could leave you in a very embarrassing position.

When you are 2 full running strides ahead of the runner,

Do your passing when coming out of a turn or on a straightaway.

Mark Belger—"Running shouldn't be the
only thing in a youngster's life."

Mark Belger
Athletic Attic

U.S. Indoor Record, 800 Meters (11-lap track), 1978 (1:48.1)
U.S. Olympic Invitational Champion, 800 Meters, 1978, 1979

A young runner, age 12 or 13, say, should train for events like the 1,000 yards and longer only by jogging. He should jog every day for 15 minutes, making up his own mind about how much distance to cover. He should always try to run at the same time of day. Make it habit. I don't like to suggest that a kid run every day. A young person is likely to find that boring. You don't want to *make* a youngster train. Some parents do. Parents can be a problem.

When a young person boy or girl gets to be 15 or so, he or she will be training under a coach and be involved in a highly structured program. But in the years before that takes place, all you want to do is work to develop the child's cardio-vascular system. Some coaches try to do more. They run a kid too fast. They burn the hell out of him, physically and mentally. You want to bring a youngster along slowly. Look at it like this. A runner doesn't reach his peak until he's around 25 years old. So if you're working with a kid of 13, say, then you're talking about a 12-year training program.

Running shouldn't be the only thing in a youngster's life. I think a youngster is more likely to stay interested in running if it's just one of several interests he or she has. I have a younger sister; she's 12. Her name is Suzanne. I think she could become the best runner in the family. The first time we ever jogged together, we covered three miles. She ran the first mile in 10 minutes, the second mile in 10 minutes, and the third mile in 10 minutes — with a kick! She has tremendous potential. But we try to cater to other interests she has. She also likes skateboarding. She rides a unicycle. She showed an interest in painting, so we bought her some paints. Because she's interested in so many different things, I think she's more likely to keep interested in running.

cut back into the inside lane. But don't relax. Stay in high gear, putting as much distance as you can between yourself and the opponent. Slow down and the opponent may decide to overtake *you*.

There may be times you have to pass on a curve. You may be in a race in which the pace is unusually slow. To pick it up, you move to the outside on a curve, roaring past runners as you come into the straightaway. Or you may find it necessary to pass on the next-to-last curve in a race in order to prevent yourself from being boxed in. Or you may find yourself in a "do or die" situation on the next to last or the last curve. But, as a general rule, it's best to pass on a straight.

Preventing someone from passing you is not an easy matter, especially if the runner comes at you without warning. The natural defense is to speed up and try to contest the pass for as long as you can. At least try to reach the curve ahead without being passed. On a curve, you'll be covering less distance than your rival and the advantage may swing in your favor.

I was very close to the finish line for the running of the Wanamaker Mile in 1979, and I watched in awe as Eamonn Coghlan, the Irish Olympian, sped through the fastest mile in Madison Square Garden history — 3:55. Just before he hit the tape, Coghlan glanced over his right shoulder. He admitted after that the glance cost him the world indoor record —

Don Paige
Villanova University

Winner, 1,000-yard run (2:05.3), Millrose Games, 1979
Winner, 1-mile run (3:56.3), International Freedom Games, 1979

When you're in high school, a freshman, say, it's very important to have respect for your coach, to listen to what he has to say, and, basically, obey him. Remember, you're new in the field, while he's got experience. He has seen and knows how to train all types of runners. Later, when you're in college, you can apply your own philosophy to what your coach has to say, but in high school you should be more inclined to follow the training program set up for you.

Coghlan sets the pace in the Wanamaker Mile.

3:54.9 at the time. "I don't know why I did it," he said. "Usually I run through the tape."

That's what to remember about the finish—run through the tape. (Just a week later, at the San Diego Invitational Games, Coghlan managed to remember it, and struck the tape in 3:52.6, tearing 2.3 seconds from Buerkle's record.) Always pretend the finish line is five or ten yards beyond, and don't slacken your pace.

1,500 METERS (1 MILE)

In the final analysis, there are two ways to win a race of 1,500 meters. You can dart into the lead early and then stay there,

Coghlan exults after winning Wanamaker mile.

or you can run off the pace, saving yourself for a final surge to the tape.

The difference between an 800 meter race and one of 1,500 meters is that in the last named you can't let yourself lose contact with the leaders. In the 800 meter this isn't likely to happen, as long as you maintain a reasonable pace. But at

1,500 meters you can slip so far behind that you'll never be able to make up the distance.

In the 1,500, you have more of an opportunity to settle down and analyze what's happening. The field seldom gets bunched, as often happens at 800 meters. Keep cool. Don't dart in and out, trying to challenge any runner who makes a move. Only in the final lap, in the back straight of the final lap, to be precise, is it important to cover challenges.

If your strategy is to run in front all the way, you gain certain immediate advantages. It's you who decides what the pace is going to be; you can make it as fast as you want. And you don't have to worry about getting boxed in for you can put about as much distance as you want between yourself and your rivals. Some individuals don't really care about such advantages. They just know they run better when there are other runners trying to catch them.

Billy Martin
Iona College

New York Metropolitan Champion, 1,000 yards, 1978 (2:11.1)
Division I All American, 1976, 1978, 1979

There are no secrets, no shortcuts toward becoming a winner in the half-mile or mile. It's pretty much a matter of miles, of how much running you're willing to do in training. As a college runner, you have your AMs and your PMs—your morning workouts and your afternoon workouts. The morning workout, usually five days a week, is distance running, maybe five to seven miles every day. In the afternoons, you do interval work or something similar, or perhaps more distance running. It depends on your event.

In the East, where the track and field year is more or less divided into three seasons—cross country in the fall, followed by the indoor season, and, last, the outdoor season in the spring—your training might also include weight work in the fall and during the winter as you build up a fitness base for the important events of the outdoor season in the spring. It's a year-round program. No one becomes a superstar overnight.

But there are some disadvantages to this strategy. Since you can't keep an eye on your opponents, there is a danger you can be passed suddenly and without warning. At outdoor meets, the pace setter can be hampered by the wind. Indeed, for those runners just behind him, he serves as a wind break. It makes the lead runner feel like he's doing all the work, and, in fact, he is.

To win, the front runner has to get so far ahead that it becomes impossible for anyone to catch him. Or he has to set such a fast pace that those who trail have nothing in reserve, and are unable to kick with any hope of success. A third alternative is for the leader to hold a little something in reserve himself, and accelerate as the race enters its final stages.

Few runners follow the strategy of leading from start to finish. One reason is because only one man has the opportunity to do so in each race. If there are 14 starters, 13 of them are going to have to use come-from-behind tactics. Also, it's easier for an individual to run off the pace. All you really have to do is keep within striking distance, waiting for the right moment to launch your attack. There is also a benefit when it comes to passing. You can shoot by a rival and be several strides ahead of him before he realizes it.

The fateful moments in the 1,500 come in the back straightaway of the final lap. As in the 800 meters, you can't let yourself be boxed in as you come out of the next-to-last curve. You have to be free to make whatever moves happens to be necessary at the time.

What you do at that point depends largely upon the pace. If you've had to extend yourself to keep up with the leaders, delay your final thrust as long as you can. If, on the other hand, you feel you have a good amount of reserve energy, draw out the opposition by attacking as you enter the back straight.

Of course, your strategy also depends on the strategy of your opponents, at least to some extent. It pays to know what each is capable of doing and the running style of each. Sometimes a rival coach may enter a 400-meter specialist in a distance race. The man takes the lead at the start and pounds out a torrid pace. But not for very long. He soon drops to the rear. The only reason for his presence is to cause opposing runners to exert themselves too much too soon in an effort to keep up. You can't let yourself be fooled by such tactics.

What turned out to be a record mile was run at the San Diego Sports Arena in 1979. What happened is interesting, not so much because of the record, but because the race matched the two opposing strategies in a classic manner. Paul Cummings, a graduate of Brigham Young University, was the pace setter. Cummings invariably ran so hard and built up so big a lead he could not be overcome. Often he would manage to bring the field to the brink of exhaustion with still a lap or so to run. His chief rival was Eamonn Coghlan, a native of Dublin, Ireland, who had raced with distinction for Villanova, having lost only one indoor mile in seven years. Coghlan

Gayle Barron
Atlanta, Georgia
Winner, Boston Marathon, 1978

People today tend to overdo. This applies especially, I think, to distance runners and the training they do. They not only work hard, but too hard. Some individuals simply aren't capable of coping with a training program that is based on high mileage. But they try it, nevertheless.

What you should do, instead, is develop a training program that suits your physical make-up, your stamina, and your ability as a runner. Don't let yourself be concerned by what other runners are doing.

By trial and error, find out what works for you — what stretching exercises are the most effective, and what amount of running you should be doing when you train, whether it be one mile, five miles, or more.

Learn to listen to your body. It will tell you when you've done enough work. Once you decide upon a program that works for you, stick with it; don't change.

was the come-from-behind specialist, a "consummate kicker," *Sports Illustrated* called him.

It was Cummings who had set the early pace in the Wanamaker mile, run just a week before, and won by Coghlan, and Cummings was also the pace setter during the last half of John Walker's indoor world-record 1,500-meter effort — 3:37.4 — at the Muhammad Ali meet the previous January. At San Diego, Cummings was jarred at the start, broke stride, and was passed by most of the field. But not long after the first quarter mark had been passed, Cummings swung into the lead. Coghlan was right behind him, calm and relaxed. "There was no point to anything but staying relaxed," Coghlan was to say later, "and letting Paul do all the work."

At the half mile, Cummings continued to lead, the rising shouts from the crowd urging him on. Coghlan was still second. Steve Scott, a twenty-two-year-old Californian, was a close third, and Wisconsin's Steve Lacy was in fourth place. As they approached the third quarter, Cummings continued to drive himself without letup, but Coghlan, Scott, and Lacy managed to cling to him.

Then Lacy turned on more speed, passing Scott and taking aim at Coghlan. When he reached his shoulder, Coghlan exploded away. How did Coghlan know it was time to make his move? "Something," he said, "comes on me and tells me to go *now*. Sometimes it may not be until the last straight. Other times — as tonight — it's with a full quarter to go. Frankly, it's a mystery."

Not long after he bolted into the lead, Coghlan was challenged by Scott. But he had something left to meet the challenge, and burst away from the American.

As he came down to the tape, Coghlan was thinking of the Wanamaker mile the week before, and how easing up at the very end had cost him the record. This time he was blazing as he struck the tape. His time of 3:52.6 was 2.3 seconds better than the world record held by Dick Buerkle. Cummings, incidentally, finished fourth at 4:00.5, behind Scott and Lacy.

Grete Waitz
Oslo, Norway

International Cross Country Champion, 1970, 1978
Women's record holder, marathon (2:32.30)
Women's record holder, 10,000 meters (31:15.4)

If you take up distance running as a young girl and you're not successful right away, don't be disappointed. Don't give up; keep trying. It takes time. You have to realize this. Your coach has to realize it, too, and not push you too much.

Suppose you begin running in your early teens. Well, it may be two or three years before you begin winning races, and it may be ten years before you become a real star. That's the way it was with me. I started running at 13. I went a long time without ever winning anything. Then suddenly I began to get results. Now I'm real good. I am very pleased with myself.

CROSS-COUNTRY RACING

In high school and college track, long-distance running frequently means cross-country running. A cross-country race is one staged over open fields or unpaved roads. It may include park terrain, a golf course, or a bridle path. The distance covered can vary from a mile or so to as much as five miles, depending on the age of the runners.

Contestants race as members of a team. The race outcome is determined by assigning point values to the finishing places of the first five members of each team (first place equals 1 point; second place, 2 points, etc.). The team with the lowest point total is the winning team.

Because the terrain is going to be uneven, your regular running shoes may not be suitable. You may require a heavier shoe, one with more than the usual amount of padding, especially in the heel area.

Planning is often the key to success in cross-country competition. About an hour before the start, jog over the

Cross-country events are team events.

Joan Benoit
Brunswick, Maine

Winner, Boston Marathon, 1979 (2:35.15, American record)

When you're 15 or 16 and beginning to take distance running seriously, you can work out your own training program. I started running at 15. It's a good age to begin, I think. You're not vulnerable to injury then. Listen to your body. Do what it tells you to do. Some days you might want to run 1 mile hard or do some repeat quarters. Other days you'll feel like doing some distance running, 4 or 5 miles, perhaps, going at a comfortable pace. Once in a while, you might want to run against the clock. Maybe you do 5 miles in 40 minutes. Well, the next time you go out, you might try to get your time down to 39 or 38 minutes. But do this only occasionally. Keep varying the program. Your body will tell you what to do.

course at a slow pace, noting the kind of terrain you're going to be encountering, and making a mental note of the various course checkpoints. Once the race begins, you don't want to be confronted with any surprises.

Pacing is another essential ingredient. Since you don't have the benefit of measured laps or the "split" calls of a coach or teammate, you must learn how to pace yourself. This involves countless practice runs over the distance at which you'll be competing.

The start for a cross-country race is usually very crowded. Try to move up among the leaders as the race gets underway, although this shouldn't imply you should launch an all-out charge to the front. Don't expend more than 80 per cent of your effort over the first 200 or so yards. All you want to do is get clear of the other competitors so that you can see where you're going. You need to have an unobstructed view of rough terrain so you can cope with it properly. You have to have a clear run to be able to leap fences or water hazards. If you're running at someone's heels, course obstructions are going to slow you down considerably.

Craig Virgin — "Develop a training schedule of your own . . ."

Craig Virgin
Lebanon, Illinois

Winner, 10,000-meter run (27:59.2), Penn Relays, 1979
Winner (with Ellison Goodall), Trevira Ten-Mile Twosome
(46:32.7), 1979
USTFF Cross Country Champion, 1978
AAU 10,000 Meter Champion, 1978 (28:15.0)

There are as many ways to be successful as a distance runner as there are athletes. You have to develop a training schedule of your own. When I was in high school, that's what I did. I watched, I listened, I learned. I adapted what others were doing, experimenting until I found a program that suited my personality and physical characteristics. I ran from 60 to 80 miles a week, blending quality and quantity. Some runners I knew were running more than that; others, less. But that didn't matter — 60 to 80 miles was what worked for me.

Your training program also has to be tailored to your environment and the facilities you have available. I live in a flat part of the country. In Oregon, it's hilly. So my training program is different than an Oregon runner's, simply because of the differences in terrain.

The high school I went to didn't have a track, so I measured one out on the grass and another one on an asphalt road. That's where I did my training. You just have to adapt.

The most challenging cross-country courses include hilly terrain. When a steep slope looms ahead, make up your mind to attack it. Increase your speed as you near it. You want your added momentum to help carry you up the hill and over the summit. As you ascend, lean into the hill and lift your knees higher. Lengthen your strides. Pump your arms more. Try not to look at the top of the hill. This causes you to straighten up and you'll slow down as a result.

Keep up your momentum on the downhill side. To maintain your balance, take shorter steps and keep more upright.

On uphill terrain, pump your arms more; lift your knees higher.

Young runners do compete in races longer than 3 miles occasionally, but there is mounting evidence it's not very wise for them to do so. Long races are simply too punishing for young bodies. As Marty Liquori, one of the country's premier distance runners of recent years, once observed, "A road runner can start the summer 6-feet tall and finish at 5-foot-6."

Young boys and girls even turn up as entrants in races of the official marathon distance, which is 26 miles, 385 yards. This is worse than unwise. Bob Campbell, chairman of the Long Distance Committee of the Road Runners Club of America, highly regarded as a coach of young long-distance runners, says that eighteen should be the minimum age for anyone attempting a race of marathon distance. Campbell advises that high-school half milers, milers, and two milers with ambitions as marathoners, gradually increase their distance work, but as complement to their speed work. Bill Rodgers, Frank Shorter, Garry Bjorklund, and Tom Fleming, often cited as the outstanding marathoners of recent years, all moved up to the marathon distance after first developing their speed at shorter distances in interscholastic and intercollegiate competition.

6

Relay Races

A relay is a race between teams, normally with four members to a team. It is run in four stages, called legs, with each member of each team running one leg. The runner finishing one leg passes a baton to the next runner, the exchange taking place within a well defined zone.

The tube-like baton is about a foot long. It can be made of metal, plastic, or wood, and it weighs a bit less than two ounces.

The standard relay races are as follows:

> 440-yard relay (four legs of 110 yards)
> 880-yard relay (4 × 220)
> 1-mile relay (4 × 440)
> 2-mile relay (4 × 880)

There are also medley relays, relays in which the legs are of unequal length. In high school competition, one popular medley relay has legs of 110, 220, 440, and 880 yards.

Running speed, technique, and tactical skill are all important toward achieving success in relay races, but deft baton passing is absolutely vital. It used to be that the oncoming runner in a relay race merely had to touch the relief runner's hand. But officials weren't always able to judge when actual hand-to-hand contact had occurred, so the passing of the baton was introduced. Through the years, the technique of passing has developed into an advanced art.

The transfer is made within a passing zone that is 22 meters (about 20 yards) in length, marked by horizontal lines. If the baton is dropped within the passing zone, either runner is permitted to retrieve it. If it is dropped outside the zone, only the runner who was carrying it can retrieve it. Actually, since a dropped baton usually spells disaster, it doesn't make much difference who does the retrieving.

Your coach will designate which hand members of your team are to use in passing and receiving the baton. The fastest method involves a right-to-left-to-right-to-left exchange. The first runner, carrying the baton in his right hand, passes it to the left hand of the second runner, who passes it to the right

Relay exchange point is often frantic scene.

hand of the third man. The final exchange is from the third man's right hand to the fourth man's left hand.

Once the outgoing runner has the baton in his grasp, he keeps it in that hand. There's no switching hands while running, not in the sprints. Switching tends to slow you down. You've got to concentrate on *running*. If it's awkward for you to receive and carry the baton in your left hand, the coach may change the running sequence of your team members to enable you to receive with your right hand, or he may assign you to run first, in which case you won't have to do any receiving at all.

To understand why this system of exchange is important, visualize how a sprint relay is run. I'm talking about 4 legs, each leg 110 yards, or one full circuit of the track. The first runner has a curve to negotiate, so he must carry the baton in his right hand, and this helps him in pumping his right arm across his body. This, in turn, aids him in leaning into the turn.

As the first man comes out of the turn, he passes to the second man, who runs his 110 on the back straightaway. The exchange puts the baton in the second man's left hand. The third exchange is from left hand to right hand, because the third man runs a curve. The fourth man, carrying the baton in his left hand, sprints through the front straightaway to the tape.

In the 440- and 880-yard relays, there's a 10-meter starting zone marked on the track just forward of the 20-meter passing zone. The runner who is to receive the baton is permitted to take up his stance position in the starting zone, and use it when accelerating. But the exchange itself has to take place in the exchange zone.

The incoming runner is responsible for the completion of the pass. Members of each team establish checkpoints on the track before the race. These checkpoints are located 5 or 6 strides short of the passing zone. When the incoming runner reaches a checkpoint, he shouts, "Go!" and the outgoing run-

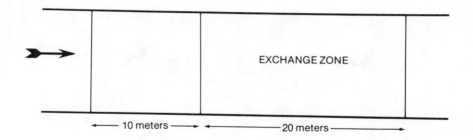

ner takes off. When both runners are traveling in high gear, and the speed of the outgoing runner blends with that of the incoming runner, the exchange is made. It should take place as early as possible in the passing zone; then, if there's fumbling, the runners have a chance to cope with it.

If you're the incoming runner, drive into the passing zone at top speed. Slowing down is a common mistake.

The actual exchange comes on a signal from the incoming runner. Shout out, "Hand!" or "Now!" When the outgoing runner hears your command, he sweeps his arm back and opens his fingers, giving you a target. Most runners today use an upsweep motion in placing the baton in the runner's hand, but some coaches prefer an overhand motion. Whichever one you use, lay the baton across the hand into the V formed by the thumb and forefinger. Be sure it's the top half of the baton that you place there. This will give the outgoing runner plenty of grasping room. It also assures that he'll be able to make *his* pass with facility. If you place the baton so the outgoing runner has to grasp it at the center, he will have to adjust his grip before making his pass, and adjusting can cost a second or two.

After the pass has been completed, stay in your lane until you've checked traffic conditions. If you cross in front of an oncoming opponent as you're leaving the track, and there's a collision, someone could get injured. You're also liable to be disqualified.

Passers and receivers have to practice constantly until

Don't slow down as you enter the exchange zone.

Sprint exchange is sometimes called "blind" exchange.

their exchange is perfectly coordinated. They have to assure that the motions used in passing and receiving are natural motions, simply, exaggerations of what they're doing normally as they sprint. When your right arm drops back to receive the baton, it does so as you're striding on your left foot. And when you sweep your right hand forward to make a pass, you do so when you're taking a stride with your left foot. In other words, you never adjust your sprinting rhythm to make a pass. Do so and it will be harmful in terms of lost speed.

To get a smooth exchange, you have to know exactly how long it is going to take your receiver to put his hand up as a target after you've said, "Now!" Practice with your receiver at a jog, and gradually increase your speed. There will be times, of course, that your coach will have all four

Hold the baton by its lower half as you run.

members of the team, working together, jogging while practicing the right-left-right-left passing sequence.

In distance relays, the baton exchange, while still important, is not crucial. The sprint exchange is sometimes referred to as a blind pass, because the receiver never gets to look at what's happening. What he does is based on the passer's shouted command and his sense of touch when the baton is placed in his hand. But in the distance relays, the incoming runner is fatigued, and so the receiver is made responsible for the exchange. He must turn to look over his shoulder to be sure that there is no mishap as the baton is being transferred. It's called a visual exchange.

If you're the receiver, turn to face the incoming runner as he nears the passing zone. If he's carrying the baton in his right hand, you receive it in your left. Turn only with your head and shoulders as you reach back. Keep your hips facing forward and one foot positioned ahead of the other, so you can sprint away when you have the baton in your hand.

The incoming runner is supposed to extend his arm fully in offering you the stick. But sometimes he may be at the point of collapse and thus will be less than perfect in what he is supposed to do. It's up to you to judge how tired the incoming runner is, and act accordingly. Remember, your first responsibility is not to let the baton slip to the track.

If you receive the baton in your left hand, but wish to switch it to your right as you're running, do so. When you arrive at the point of exchange, there's no need to switch back, either. It's up to the receiver to adjust his body position according to the hand in which you're holding the baton.

Your coach will set the order in which members of your team are to run so as to use each runner to the greatest advantage. The runner who has the fastest start and accelerates quickest is almost certain to be assigned the lead-off position. He also has to able to pass the baton well.

The second and third runners have to be adept at handling the baton, because each of them does so twice, once as a receiver, once as a passer. It's very advantageous if the second runner man is particularly fast. A speedy second leg that

In distance relays, receiver can look back to assure trouble-free pass.

follows a good exchange and a fast start puts a great deal of pressure on the other teams. Rival runners may tense up as a result.

Traditionally, the fourth man, the anchor man, is the team's fastest sprinter. But this doesn't hold true in every case. If the coach realizes that his team's speedster excels because he's good coming out of the blocks, he may ask him to lead off. Or if the man is skilled at passing the baton, but not so skilled in receiving it, the coach may reconsider about having him anchor.

Another consideration is whether the team's fastest runner has the ability to come from behind. Some speedsters don't. They're front runners. When they're in the lead, they have the ability to hold it, not permitting anyone to pass. But when they trail, they have difficulty catching up. A coach would never use a front runner in a spot where a come-from-behind specialist is likely to be needed.

7

The High Jump

To flop or not to flop? That's the decision you'll have to make when you take up this event.

The flop, or Fosbury Flop, to use its full name, was created by Dick Fosbury, a 6-foot-4 jumper from Oregon State University, who won a gold medal in the 1968 Olympics with a jump of 7'4½". In using the flop technique, you go over the bar backwards and headfirst, landing on your back. You kind of flop over, in other words.

The flop is opposed to the straddle. In this, you approach the bar at an angle, spring into the air, and clear the bar belly down, your feet apart, the bar bisecting your body.

Before trying either style, be sure to establish which foot is your natural takeoff foot. If you're right-handed, it's probably your left foot. But try this test: Get a low hurdle, and after an approach of 4 or 5 steps, bound over it. Do it 4 or 5 times. One foot will establish itself as the dominant takeoff foot. Plan to use that foot in taking off every time you jump. The pages of instructional advice that follow are written for a jumper using a left-foot takeoff.

The best jumpers spend more time refining their takeoff techniques than anything else. Much care goes into establishing the best possible takeoff point. Generally speaking, your

Debbie Brill—"The high jump should be fun . . . Just play with the event."

Debbie Brill
Los Angeles

AAU Champion, 1978
AAU Championship Record, 6'2" (1978)

When you're young and a beginner, the high jump should be fun. Just play with the event. Don't let it be the cause of stress or tension. Keep it fun as long as you can. Your talents will develop naturally. If the event becomes work, don't do it. You've got plenty of years ahead of you.

takeoff foot should be about one arm's length from the bar when you plant it down. Through trial and error, you'll undoubtedly want to adjust this distance an inch or so forward or back, however.

The standard procedure is to mark one's takeoff point with a piece of tape, and put another piece of tape at the starting point of the approach. If, as you approach, you realize that you're not going to hit the tape at the takeoff point with your takeoff foot, pull up. Go back and start again. There's no penalty. As long as no part of your body crosses over or under the bar, you can use as many approaches as you want.

Some jumpers establish other check marks besides those at the start and the takeoff mark. A jumper will put a piece of tape where his fourth step should strike, for instance, or his fifth or sixth step, or, in the case of the Fosbury Flop, where he should begin circling toward the bar. Be wary about doing this, however. You don't want to get too involved in checkpoints. You need one at the start. You need one to mark your takeoff point. But it's moot whether you need any others. Jumping is what you should be concentrating on as you approach. Check marks should be secondary. They shouldn't become an event in themselves.

In the high jump (and also in the triple jump and the pole vault), as soon as a competitor clears one height, he gets three chances to clear the next height. Sometimes the next height is designated by the officials and other times by the contestants.

To conserve energy, a jumper may wish to pass up a turn. He is permitted to do so, but he is credited only with the last height he actually cleared. The competitor who clears the highest level wins. If two or more competitors are eliminated at the same height, the one with the fewest misses is declared the winner.

Many high jumpers wear special shoes. They have two spikes in the heels. When you approach the bar and plant the takeoff foot, you plant it heel first. The spikes help prevent slipping.

While you have to work constantly toward improving your technique, your training program should also include some sprint work and even some hurdling. Sprinting will build your approach speed. Hurdling improves the suppleness of your legs.

Be careful about too much practice jumping. High jumping is an event in which you can easily leave your best effort on the practice field. Some coaches do not permit their athletes to practice jump more than once or twice a week.

THE FLOP

Debbie Brill, a champion high jumper, jumped 6'1¼" as a teen-ager, and she used the flop. "That bar is gruesome to look at," she once said. "So I turn my back on it, and this gives me a psychological boost."

The flop approach.

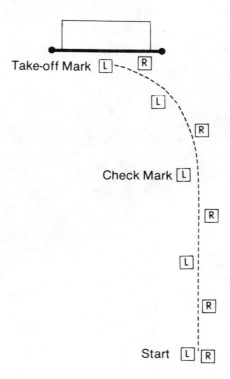

In the flop, you turn your back to the bar as you go over.

You *do* turn your back on the bar when you use the flop technique, going over headfirst. Your upper body is crossing the bar while your legs from the knee down dangle below bar level. To get the lower legs over, you must remember to kick them up. Raising the arms helps to lift the legs.

You land on your back when you use the flop, and because you do you need a foam-rubber landing pit. Sawdust, wood chips, or sand don't provide enough cushioning when you're coming down on your back. If a foam-rubber pit is not available to you, then you should learn the straddle technique, or else think about specializing in some other event.

What Dick Fosbury did in developing his jump was to take a popular jump of the day, the scissors jump, and convert it to the flop. The scissors jump is simple. Try it a few times before you try the Fosbury Flop. It's a good training exercise.

Set the crossbar at a very low height. Approach the bar slightly from one side. As you make your approach, drop both arms back. Then, as you approach your takeoff point, start swinging the arms forward, driving them as high as your shoulders.

Plant your left foot — your takeoff foot. The right leg goes over the bar first. It's almost as if you're sitting down, except your left leg is doubled back and trails. As your right leg clears the bar, snap your left leg through. You land on your right foot first, then your left.

What Fosbury did was transform the scissors. Instead of going over the bar front-side first, Fosbury presented his back and shoulders to the bar, and went over headfirst. This involved pivoting almost one-half turn on the takeoff foot just as it was planted.

It also necessitated modifying the approach. The approach for the flop contains a curve. Overall, it has rather a J shape. It can be 8, 9, or 10 strides. In the first 4 or 5 strides, you run straight for the bar, then begin circling toward it, leaning to the inside as you go. On your last 2 steps, you're striding almost parallel to the bar. As you run, you should increase your speed with each step. Think in terms of attacking the bar.

Your upper body goes over first; you have to kick your legs up.

At the takeoff, your arms drive to shoulder height. Your right knee drives upward. You rotate on the toes of your planted foot, your left foot, so that you end up facing away from the bar. At the same time, you push off.

When you're in the air, your body continues turning. Lean back with your upper body. Tuck your chin to your chest and then turn your head so as to look over your shoulder at the bar.

Keep your arms close to your sides as you go over. As your upper body clears the bar, lift your feet. Lift your arms, too, because this helps in getting your lower legs over.

You'll come down on your shoulders and upper back.

Relax; spreading your arms will help to cushion the impact.

The technique involved in the flop is not difficult to learn. What may present a problem is adjusting to the feeling of taking off backwards, then soaring upside down and headfirst through the air. This is not something that the average person does with any degree of regularity. But with practice you'll get used to it, and peering over your shoulder toward the bar and then the pit helps in alleviating your anxiety.

Start with the bar at a low level, and increase the height gradually. The same with your approach speed. Don't try to set any speed records at first. You do want to be aggressive in your approach, of course, but not immediately. Increase your speed as the level of your jumps gets higher.

It may take you some time to determine the number of

You land on your shoulders and upper body.

approach steps that are right for you. Try 8 steps at first, then add another, and if that doesn't feel right, try adding one more.

If you have a tendency to hit the bar with your shoulder on the way up, it means you're reaching your maximum height too late; you're taking off too close to the bar. Adjust your takeoff spot and starting point accordingly. (To establish your starting point, run your approach in reverse from your takeoff mark.)

If you keep hitting the bar with your shoulders on the way down, it indicates that you're reaching your maximum height too soon. Your takeoff point is too far from the bar.

As you gain experience and skill in jumping, you'll also have to adjust your takeoff point. Greater height in your jumps means your takeoff point has to be a longer distance from the bar.

Franklin Jacobs, the best of present-day American jumpers, has a technique that resembles the Fosbury Flop, but the resemblance is slight. He calls his style the Jacobs Slop. It begins with a 13-step, curving approach. As he reaches the bar, Jacobs hurls himself upward, throws his arms straight back over his head, arches his back, then goes careening over. Coaches shake their heads in dismay at Jacobs' lack of technical excellence. But he manages to do what has to be done.

Franklin Jacobs
Fairleigh Dickinson University
American Indoor High Jump Record Holder (7'7¼"), 1978

When you're young and just beginning, you have a dream, an unrealistic dream, of what you can achieve. Well, follow that dream. Hold onto it. Don't let it disappear. That's the way I felt. What's happened is a dream come true.

Newspapers sometimes refer to Franklin (he doesn't like to be called Frank) as The Human Spring. He gets his springiness from very powerful thigh muscles. "Most high jumpers' front thighs are flexible," Franklin once noted. "But mine are hard. Very tight. Some jumpers do exercises to stretch that muscle. But I don't bother about it at all."

Another distinction that Franklin has is his height — or lack of it. High jumpers are almost always very tall. Franklin stands 5'8½", which is at least seven inches shorter than Vladimir Yashchenko of the Soviet Union, holder of the indoor record.

Franklin recalls once meeting the towering Wilt Chamberlain, one of pro basketball's all-time greats. Chamberlain was 7'2½". Standing next to Chamberlain was like standing next to a lamppost. But Wilt was impressed by Franklin and looked down at him and said, "Little brother, you could jump over me!"

THE STRADDLE

To straddle, says the dictionary, means to sit with the legs wide apart (as when on horseback), and that pretty much describes the position of the jumper's body when this high-jumping technique is used. You have a leg on either side of the bar as you attempt to maneuver your head and upper body over it.

Plan an approach of 7 or 8 steps, increasing your speed with each step. Approach the bar from the left side at about a 45-degree angle (this presupposes your left foot is your takeoff foot).

With your approach and takeoff, you want to thrust your upper body upward, not on a plane that is parallel with the bar. You create this upward thrust when you plant your takeoff foot. Drive upward with both arms. Drive upward with your lead knee — your right knee.

Your right hand and arm clear the bar first. Your upper

body is parallel to the bar; you're stomach-down. Bring your trailing arm—your left arm—to your side.

It's at this point that jumpers face their greatest problem —getting the trailing leg to clear the bar. This is true of top-flight jumpers as well as beginners. One way to help avoid having your trailing leg nudge the bar off the pins is to turn your head as you clear the bar; turn it so you're looking back at your takeoff spot. As you turn your head, your body tends to follow, which works to elevate the trailing leg, and also to straighten it, and thereby get it over the bar.

Continue this slow roll as you drop toward the pit. When you land, you should land on your shoulders and the upper part of your back, and you should be looking up into the sky (or toward the girders that support the roof).

The Western roll is another high-jumping technique. It's similar to the straddle. When you go over the bar using the

The straddle approach.

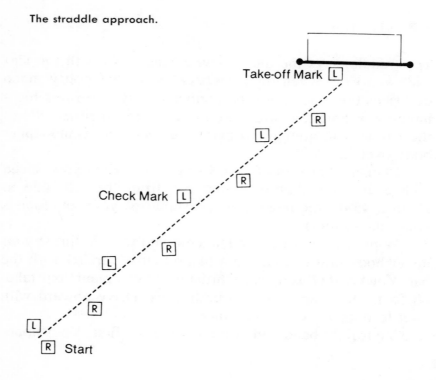

In the straddle, you have a leg on either side of the bar as you go over.

straddle, you're belly down. But in the Western roll, you're lying on your side as you clear the bar, and your takeoff leg, the left leg, is tucked under the lead leg. The approach is the same as in the straddle.

While most high jumpers today are using the flop, or their own rendition of it, the straddle style is not dead. Far from it. The Soviet Union's Vladimir Yashchenko, who set the world outdoor record in 1977 by jumping 7'7¾", is a straddler. A tall man—6'4"—Yashchenko approaches the bar deliberately, almost as if he was trying to sneak up on it. Even his last few strides are taken at somewhat less than full speed.

Valery Brumel, another world record holder for the Soviets, and the winner of an Olympic gold medal in 1964, also used the straddle. Most Americans of Brumel's day walked up to the bar, but Brumel raced to it. He could run the 100-yard dash in 9.8 seconds. Not only was he a speedster, but he was very strong, and he used his strength to convert his great speed into upward thrust. When Fosbury was developing his flop, he patterned his fast approach after that of Brumel's.

Which is best, the straddle or the flop? Most coaches believe that the flop is easiest to learn. Nevertheless, there's a lingering fondness for the straddle among American coaches. Frank Costello, track coach at the University of Maryland, admits that straddle jumping is almost a lost art. As he travels about seeking recruits, he finds very few high-school straddlers. But he believes that the straddle is the superior style, that it permits greater technical improvement. "It's a great technique," he says, "but it has to be taught correctly, the way the Soviets teach it."

8

The Long Jump

Aside from running itself, the running long jump is probably the most natural of all events. Hopscotch and other school-yard games are based on long jumping. Nevertheless, championship competition in the running long jump, whether at the Olympic level or in high school, demands lightning speed in the approach, split-second timing in the takeoff, and the development of refined techniques in "flying" and landing.

The idea of the event, of course, is to leap as far as possible. The distance of your jump is measured from the pit-side of the takeoff board to the nearest mark in the sand made by any part of your body.

While your ambition is to jump for distance, your immediate aim as you sprint down the runway and spring into the air should be to jump for height. The higher you jump, the more time you'll spend in the air, and the longer you're in the air, the more you'll be able to take advantage of the momentum created by your run.

In other words, go fast and go high. Do both and you'll go far.

You can make your approach as long or as short as you want. It depends on how long it takes you to reach your greatest speed from a standing start. It can be anywhere from 80 to 120 feet. To determine how far your approach should be, stand at the takeoff board and run back from it, accelerating until you're sprinting your fastest. Have someone mark the spot where you first reach maximum speed. Use that as your starting spot.

On each jump, your takeoff foot must strike the board in exactly the same manner, with the toes touching the board itself. Your approach must bring you to your takeoff mark with your foot in this position on every jump attempt. What this means is that you have to be consistent with your approach steps. Establishing checkpoints along the approach will help you to develop this consistency. Some jumpers put down checkmarks for each one of several of their strides. For example, a jumper might use the 2-4-10 plan, establishing checkmarks where his toes should strike on the second, fourth, and tenth steps. Other jumpers use a 2-4-8 plan.

As you sprint through your approach, keep your upper body erect. In the last few steps, begin preparing for the take-

---

Larry Myricks
Mississippi Southern College
AAU Champion, 1979, 1976

A lot of this event is mental. Young jumpers can get frustrated by it, and they get discouraged as a result. You've got to hit the takeoff board, and you've got to hit it right. Sometimes a young jumper might not be exactly on it; he'll be over it or he'll be behind it. This throws him off. He can't understand what's happening. He loses his confidence.

I try not to let things like that bother me. Normally, I take an approach of 127 feet, 5 inches. If I run that distance twice and I miss the board both times, I don't let it get to me. I realize that you don't run the same everyday. Every track is different. So I just change my approach distance, making it shorter or longer. You got to take it easy. You got to be able to adjust.

Drive from the takeoff board.

Takeoff Mark [L]
[R]
[L]
[R]
Check Mark [L]
[R]
[L]
[R]
[L]
[R]
Start [L] [R]

off, thrusting your chest forward, raising your chin.

As you approach, keep your eyes focused on the board. But as soon as you're confident that your takeoff foot is going to strike down at the right spot, shift your gaze toward the horizon.

The takeoff foot should strike gently. If you come down too hard, you can kill your forward momentum. You don't want to lose even the tiniest amount of speed.

Your body should be erect as you hit the board, your chest forward, your chin up. Drive your lead knee upward to get as much height as you can. Drive upward with both arms, too.

Martha Watson
Los Angeles Track Club

World Indoor Record, 1973 (21'4¾")
AAU Champion, 1976, 1975, 1974, 1967

Learn your event. Learn it like you're training to become a coach. If you have a good coach, and he tells you what to do and how to do it, you can get to depend on him too much. Ask questions; find out *why*. In a meet when you're competing, the coach isn't going to be there to give you advice. You're on your own. You have only yourself.

Many beginners believe that various gyrations they perform in the air will make them go farther. Not true. There are at least two different methods of using the arms and legs between takeoff and landing, but the chief purpose of this movement is to prepare the body for landing. It does nothing toward increasing the length of your flight.

There are two ways of using your body in the air. They are called the hang and the hitch-kick.

The hang is the easier of the two. Recall, as you take off, your chest is thrust forward, your chin is up. Your back should be slightly arched. As you approach the midpoint of the jump, bring your trailing leg alongside your lead leg; keep your knees slightly bent. Raise your arms over your head. Your body position now resembles that of a gymnast hanging from a trapeze.

As you apporach the point of touch-down, snap your legs

The hang is easier than the hitch-kick.

forward and your arms downward. In other words, you go from the trapeze position to almost a sitting position.

In the hitch-kick, the jumper looks as if he is walking in the air. You actually take a stride-and-a-half before you land. As you take off, you bring your takeoff leg forward and thrust your lead leg back. This is the full stride. Then you bring the lead leg forward, but only a half a stride. Now both of your legs should be extended in front of you — you're in about a sitting position — ready for landing.

The idea of the landing is touch down with both feet as far forward as possible, and then to fall forward. If you fall back, the length of your jump will be measured from the impression made by your hands as you put them behind your body to keep from falling over. In other words, you'll slice two or three feet from the length of your jump.

To help prevent this, when you extend your legs, spread your feet about 12 inches apart. When you do this, you create the space your body needs to swing forward. As soon as your heels make contact, swing your arms forward past your feet. This will increase the forward thrust of your body.

The most important thing to remember in long jumping is to get *up* as well as out at the point of takeoff. To get into the habit of jumping high, have a pair of teammates hold a length of string about 2½ to 3 feet above the takeoff board. Concentrate on getting your feet over the string on a series of practice jumps.

Sprinting and hurdling drills are both recommended for long jumpers. Sprinting is good because it helps to build your approach speed. Hurdling will help you to develop the precise strides you need in your approach. You have to be able to hit the takeoff board with your toes without actually having to look at it.

As in the high jump, you can't do too many long jumps in any given practice session. You can work on your approach, on hitting your checkmarks precisely as you race down the runway. You can work on getting height into your jump by taking very short approaches, hitting your takeoff spot, and

Snap your legs forward as you get set to land.

leaping high. But be careful about overdoing the long jump it-self.

Because this event places extra pressure on the heel as you take off, you may want to insert a plastic heel cup inside the shoe of your takeoff foot. This will give you support and protection that the ordinary racing flat does not provide. After the event is over, the heel cup can be removed. The triple jump is another event in which a heel cup is sometimes used.

A plastic insert will help protect and support your heel.

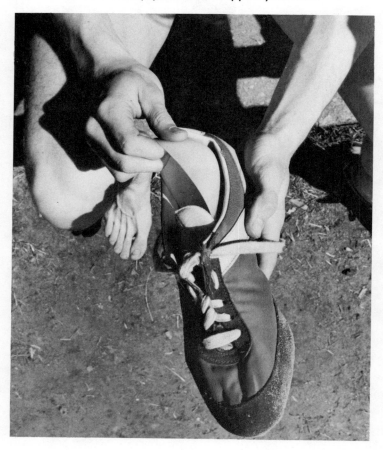

9

The Triple Jump

The triple jump used to be called the hop, step, and jump. While the name has been changed, the various phases of the event are still referred to in those terms. Each competitor jumps for distance from a running start, landing first on the takeoff foot (a hop), then on the other foot (a step), and last, on both feet (a jump). It is similar in many ways to the long jump, but whereas the long jumper tries to go as far as he can on one bound, the triple jumper tries for distance with three different bounds.

The event is conducted on the standard long-jump runway and using the same landing pit. The difference is that the takeoff board is set farther back on the runway, so the hop and step portions are performed on solid ground. Establish approach and takeoff checkpoints for yourself, just as long jumpers do (see previous section).

The triple jump is not an easy event to master. It has been included in high school track-and-field programs for only a relatively short time, since 1964. Each of your landings must propel you forward toward the next phase. If a landing should work to slow you down, you won't do well in this event. Think of your body as a flat stone ricocheting over the surface of a smooth pond. It skips from one point to the next, keeping low, maintaining much of its forward momentum between skips. Have that image in your mind as you approach this event.

One thing you must do to achieve a skimming effect is to put exactly the same amount of effort into each phase of the event. You can't emphasize the hop phase more than the step phase, or stress either the hop or the step more than the jump. You have to give equal treatment to each; otherwise, you won't have the overall smoothness and rhythm needed for a winning distance.

In the hop phase, use your strongest leg as your takeoff leg.

The hop, the first phase of the event, is executed from the takeoff board, using the same approach as the long-jumper's approach. Use your strongest leg as your takeoff leg because it must take the strain of two consecutive landings and takeoffs. Hit the board with the toes of the takeoff foot, but, instead of soaring high as in the long jump, strive to keep lower to the ground (like that skimming stone).

As you take off, raise both arms. Drive forward with your chest and the knee of your lead leg.

While you're in midair, swing the takeoff leg forward, keeping the knee bent so it will be ready to cushion your landing. The other leg swings back.

If you use the left foot in taking off in the hop phase, you use it again in taking off in the step phase. Use your arms to help drive you forward as you take off. Drive your right leg forward, too. It's a takeoff that's the same as the takeoff you used in the hop phase, only this time you should be leaning more forward, bounding toward the pit end of the runway.

As you step, use your arms to help you get height and distance.

Tommy Haynes—"Work on even phases . . . make all your steps the same size."

Tommy Haynes
New York Pioneer Track Club

U.S. Indoor Record, 1976 (55´5½˝)
AAU Champion, 1977, 1976, 1975

Work on even phases; that is, make all your steps the same size, say, three yards. Just because the step phase is short, you shouldn't shorten your steps.

Young jumpers should also work on hop-step combinations. Youngsters usually have a good hop but a poor step. They go too high with it. Working on the hop and step together helps to overcome this fault.

As you approach the second landing, draw your arms back and bend your right knee as you prepare to land on your right foot. After you've landed and are driving off your right foot, swing your arms forward. Try to get as much height as you can into your jump. Bring your left leg alongside your right. Keep your body in a hang position. There won't be time to perform a hitch-kick (see previous section).

Just before you land, swing your arms back and thrust your feet forward. Keep your feet high. Land in the same way a long jumper lands, swinging your hands forward over your feet.

In a jump of 50 feet (which is about 2 feet less than the high school record), the hop phase is about 18 feet in length; the step, 15 feet; and the jump, 17 feet. But these statistics can vary widely, depending on the jumper and his style and technique. The important thing to remember is to blend the three phases into a smooth and rhythmic whole.

In your first attempts in this event, try triple jumping from a standing-still position; that is, without any approach run. When you feel you've developed the basic rhythm of the three phases, then start adding approach steps.

Training for the triple jump is similar to long-jump training. Sprinting and hurdling drills are recommended. Be careful about overjumping in practice sessions.

Thrust your feet forward as you get set to land.

10

The Pole Vault

The first poles used in vaulting competition were made of bamboo, and then came aluminum. Anytime a vaulter went higher than 14', he was hailed far and wide. Fiber glass poles, introduced in the 1960s, changed all. High schoolers were soon exceeding 16 feet and doing it with startling regularity. The fiber glass pole has much more spring to it. It creates a catapult action that actually serves to fling the vaulter upward and over the bar.

This doesn't mean that technique is not important. In order to get the most out of the pole, you need to generate good running speed in your approach. You have to ram the pole into the vaulting box forcefully and with perfect timing. You need shoulder and arm strength to be able to pull yourself up. You need delicate body control once you're being lifted to be able to cross the bar and disengage yourself from the pole. Most vaulters are rather tall, powerfully built, and acrobatic athletes.

Choose your pole carefully, weighing all the variables. Take, for example, the pole used by UCLA's Mike Tully, who set the world indoor record in 1978 with a vault of 18'5¼". Tully's pole was an AMF Voit Pacer III 500/88,

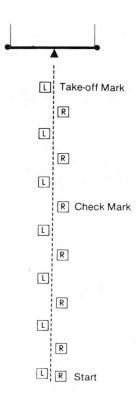

one of fifty-two different models offered by Voit at the time. The 500 was a reference to the pole's length in centimeters (about 16.4 feet). The 88 meant 88 kilos (about 194 pounds), the amount of weight the pole was capable of supporting. A vaulter weighing more than 194 pounds could snap the pole. A warning label on the pole read: "The weight specified on this pole is the maximum which should not be exceeded."

Tully's pole weighed less than 6 pounds. It had a flex designation of 5.75. That meant that were the pole to be stretched out horizontal and a 50-pound weight suspended at its midpoint, the pole would sag 5.75 inches. Flex designation is a way of expressing pole flexibility. A designation of 5.75 indicates a very stiff pole, one that would have to be used by a vaulter of exceptional speed and strength. The words speed and strength describe Mike Tully. The girls in his high school class once voted him "Mr. Muscle."

Gunther Lohre
West Germany
European Champion

A beginner in pole vaulting should find someone who knows about the event, someone who can give him advice on poles. That's the first thing to do. You need to get a pole that suits your physical makeup and vaulting style, a pole that has just the right amount of stiffness. Most kids I see can choose from among only two or three poles. But you should really try out a great many of them before you make a decision.

What else is important? Running and the plant. Run fast and plant the pole right, and you'll go high. It's as simple as that.

The pole was made of 70 per cent glass and 30 per cent resin. Tully wrapped it in red, white, and blue plastic tape.

As a beginner, pick out a pole that tests 5 to 10 pounds more than your weight. It should be about 3 meters (10′) in length. A full-size pole measures 5.2 meters (17′). Poles are hollow and fitted with a rubber cup at one end which is planted in the takeoff box.

To help prevent your hands from slipping, tape the pole where your right hand grips (if you're right-handed). Use black electrician's tape, overlapping each winding so as to create a series of ridges.

Fiber glass poles tend to bend more in one direction that another. The manufacturer's label is usually pasted to the side that has the greatest degree of flexibility. You should always plant the pole so the most bendable side is away from you. To put it another way, the label side should face the pit.

As in high jumping, you need a landing pit that offers the maximum amount of cushioning. A foam pad, 2 to 3 meters thick, approximately 5 meters on each side, is frequently used. You also need supervision. Never attempt a vault without a coach or instructor close at hand.

You have to experiment somewhat to find a grip that's right.

If you're right-handed, carry the pole on the right side of your body during the approach. Position the right hand so the palm faces up; the left hand with the palm facing down. Beyond these instructions, the rules for carrying the pole are few. Develop your own gripping style by trial and error. Begin your experimentation by grasping the pole about a foot above the highest handhold you can reach. Keep your hands about 18 inches apart. As you take your approach run, you should feel you have complete control over the pole. Keep adjusting your grip until you achieve that feeling.

Your approach should be planned carefully. It has to be such that it enables you to accelerate gradually and attain the greatest possible speed. "Pole vaulting is a sprinting event," Mike Tully once said. "It's a matter of how much speed you can get on the runway. The faster you run, the higher you jump."

But you must keep in control as you run. Control is nec-

Your approach should be a sprint.

As you plant the pole, your right hand reaches for the sky.

essary in order to assure a smooth and powerful takeoff. As a beginner, try an approach of from 8 to 10 strides. Establish checkmarks at the start of your approach and at the takeoff point, which should be approximately 10 feet forward of the vaulting box. As you become skilled and experienced as a vaulter, you'll want to take a longer approach.

As you approach, keep your eyes focused on the takeoff box. Run with plenty of knee action, holding the pole close to your hip, the front tip at about eye level.

The plant and the takeoff are the critical phases of this event. You must generate enough momentum not only to be able to swing over the bar, but to bend the pole so that its springlike qualities will add to the height you achieve.

As you near the end of your approach, start raising your right hand—past your right side, past your right ear. At the same instant your foot hits the runway on the final stride of your approach, your right arm should become fully stretched, as if you were reaching for a hook suspended from the sky. It's then that you slam the pole into the back of the box.

You drive forward with your chest, hips, and right knee. The pole begins bending. Step off into the air.

At this point, your instinct is to swing forward, to pull the pole toward you. But you have to resist this temptation. Instead, you must use your lower hand to hold yourself back, keeping the pole in front of your chest. Hanging back helps you to maintain a low center of gravity which enables you to take full advantage of the spring of the pole.

As the recoiling pole begins its lifting action, begin to rock back, bringing your knees toward your shoulders and extending your legs, your feet together. The pole is now vertical and your body is in line with it. You're doing a handstand on the pole.

Now the trick is to turn your body and flip over the bar. Push hard with your left hand, then with your right. You should be looking down at the vaulting box. Drop your legs over the bar. You'll begin a slow backward somersault as you descend toward the pit. You'll land on your back.

The momentun of your approach should bend the pole, springing you over the bar.

It takes a deft touch to flip your body over the bar and disengage yourself from the pole.

As you go over, thrust your arms over your head so they won't hit the bar.

As a vaulter, you have to work constantly to improve your technique. Try to vault three times a week, striving to do your very best on each vault. If you're careless, you can easily develop serious technical faults.

Your training should also include gymnastics work. Rope exercises are especially good. Grip the rope with your left hand, jump up and grip it with your right, then jackknife your body into a vertical position. Trampoline work will help you to improve your co-ordination. On the horizontal bar, practice swinging up and over the bar with your legs and hips straight. All such drills should be done under supervision.

11

The Shot Put

For success in weight-throwing events, of which shot-putting is the foremost, you have to be big and strong. Al Feuerbach, the American shot-put champion, stands 6'1" and weighs 242 pounds. Maren Seidler, the best female shot putter in American history, is also a large and powerful person.

But sheer bulk in itself is not guarantee you'll excel. You also have to have quickness and control to be able to generate the explosive power necessary to catapult the metal ball away.

The shot is made of iron or brass, and sometimes it is covered with rubber. High school women hurl an 8-pound shot; college women, a 12-pound shot; college men, one that weighs 16 pounds (7.26 kilograms).

It is not quite accurate to say that the shot is thrown; it is put. When you put, you push; you extend your arm quickly, propelling the shot away from where it's being held near your shoulder. There's no windup as in the discus or javelin throws.

You do your putting from within a throwing circle that is 7' in diameter. There's a toeboard (also called a stopboard) at the front of the circle that is 4" high and covers an arc that is

Getting set, position the shot like this.

4' in length. The toeboard is meant to keep competitors from overstepping the circle. You can touch the side of the toeboard with your foot, but if you touch the top of it or go outside the circle it's a foul.

Extending outward at a 45-degree angle from the center of the throwing circle are two lines that form an area shaped like a slice of pie. It is called the throwing sector. The ends of the two lines are marked with small flags. The shot must land within the throwing sector in order to qualify as a legal throw.

The shot should set in your hand, resting at the base of your fingers, the thumb and little finger supporting it from the sides. If you hold the shot too low in your hand, so it rests on your palm, you won't be able to snap it away when you release. Squeeze the shot lightly for control.

When you're getting set to throw, cock your wrist and point your elbow away from your body. The back of your throwing hand should rest on your collarbone, while the shot itself

---

Sandra Burke
Northeastern University

Winner, Women's Shot Put, Penn Relays (48'9", meet record), 1979

Technique is a big thing. I threw on my own in high school; I didn't have a coach. I just followed what the men were doing and read books. As a result, my technique was bad. You have to have your hip under you when you throw. You have to use your legs. The legs are the whole thing. I never used my legs in high school. I threw with my upper body. It wasn't until I got to college that I started learning the right technique. "Legs! Legs! Legs!" my coach shouts at me during practices.

Working with weights is important, too. During my sophomore year in college, I had 4 weight-lifting sessions a week, a total of 12 hours. I did squats and dead lifts, leg bends and inclines. The clean and jerk is important, too. Everyone I know in this event is involved in weight-lifting.

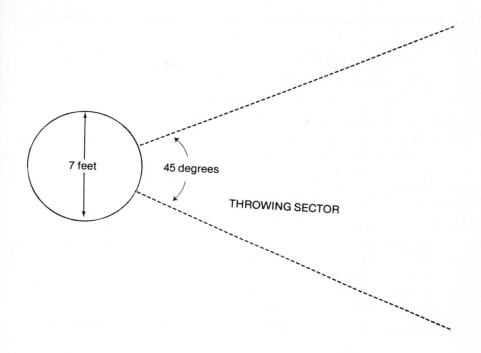

7 feet

45 degrees

THROWING SECTOR

should be in position against the neck and under the jaw. Hold your left arm out for balance.

As a beginner, put the shot from a standing position. This will give you the opportunity to develop the muscles of your arm, shoulders, and thighs at the same time you're improving your putting technique. Later, when you're able to achieve reasonable distance with a standing pat, you can try a more advanced technique, taking a backward hop and gliding across the ring to develop momentum and increase your putting distance.

For the standing put, stand with the side of your left foot against the toeboard, your right foot approaching the center of the circle. Place the back of your hand against your collar bone, with the shot against your neck and under the jaw. Bend both knees, but keep your body's weight concentrated over your right foot. You're going to shift your weight from your right foot to your left, and at the same time push hard and release the shot.

Ian Pyka
University of Maryland
IC4A Champion, 1979 (62'3", meet record)

You can't perform well in this event unless you have confidence in yourself. I'm relatively small for a shot putter. I stand 6'1"; I weigh 235. Everyone of the other leading shot putters is bigger than I am. But I never let this bother me. My coach helped me to build my confidence. You have to believe in your coach and stick to what he tells you, what he teaches you.

You have to be determined, too. You'll probably make great progress at first, but then you'll reach a plateau. You think you're going to stay there forever. When that happens, just be patient. It happens to everyone. I got stuck at 59 feet for a long time. But I kept working, kept practicing. Finally, I broke 60 feet. Then the next year I went over 61 feet. You have to mature with the sport. Too many guys give up at an early age.

Bending slightly from the waist, turn your body to the right, cocking it. Then drive in the other direction, pushing off on the right from the right foot to trigger the turn, the left arm leading. As your weight begins to shift, straighten up over your left leg, thrust your right arm up, sending the shot away.

Remember, it goes like this: lift, turn, and toss — lift with the right leg, turn the body to the left, and thrust the shot away.

The more advanced method of putting involves a low backward hop and a quick glide across the throwing circle to generate momentum. This putting technique was first used successfully by Parry O'Brien, gold medalist for the United States in the 1952 and 1956 Olympics. In fact, at one time the style was called the O'Brien Put.

Using this method, you take your stance at the back of the throwing ring; that is, on the side of the circle opposite the toeboard. Your right foot is forward; your left foot, to be the lead foot, is back. You're facing in the direction opposite to that of your throw.

Adjust the shot in your hand, positioning it against the neck and under the jaw. Bend forward from the hips, lowering your body over your right knee. Extend your left leg out behind your body. You're coiled now, ready for the launch.

Put involves quick backward hop and glide.

With your body still in the position described above, push off from your right foot and at the same time kick back with your left leg, kicking in the direction you intend to throw. The momentum you generate will pull you across the ring, your right foot ending up in about the center of the ring. You're still facing in the opposite direction of your toss.

Then, without pausing, uncoil your body. Your left foot comes to rest against the toeboard. Push off from the right foot, and start turning your hips and shoulders. When your hips and shoulders are square to the direction of the throw, the right arm begins its upward thrust, ending with the release. Your body should drive forward and upward with so much force that you're lifted onto your toes.

In final stage, you turn, drive upward, and thrust the shot away.

When you use this throwing style, what you want to work for is smoothness, on keeping the shot moving continuously from the moment you put it into motion until you release it. If there's the slightest hesitation at any point, you're going to fail in your effort to harness the momentum generated by the glide. A disappointing toss will be the result.

Think in terms of driving across the circle to an explosion point. Top-flight athletes in this event release the shot with an explosive burst of air from their lungs which is accompanied by a primitive, earsplitting grunt. It's the sound you'd hear if you whacked someone in the belly with a baseball bat.

Both standing puts and glide puts should be a part of your training program, but you shouldn't put the shot any more than two or three times a week. Jogging and wind sprints should also be included. Weight training is almost mandatory for real success in this event, but get advice from a coach or instructor before embarking on a weight program.

Jackie Gordon
University of Florida

Winner, Women's Discus Throw, Penn Relays (151'), 1979

Sometimes you get put into this event just because you're big and strong. But these characteristics are of limited value. You just can't muscle it in this event. It takes finesse. It takes technique. You have to have the right velocity and right angle of release. That's why you have to talk to somebody who really knows the event. Some coaches don't incidentally, especially in high school.

But there's a lot you can do on your own. You can go to clinics. You can study films and read books. You can go to meets and watch good discus throwers, and ask questions. When I was learning the event, I used to watch Jean Roberts, an Australian. She wasn't very big, but she was fast and efficient. The first time I met Mac Wilkins, I prepared specific questions to ask him.

Being strong is important, of course. But unless you know how to apply that strength correctly, you'll never realize your potential.

12

The Discus

In ancient Greece, discus throwing was held in the highest esteem. Not even marathon runners were honored as highly as discus artists.

The discus itself has not changed a great deal since Grecian times. Made of wood and rimmed in metal, it looks like a pair of pie plates that have been joined together, top to top. In men's high school competition, the discus weighs 3 pounds, 9 ounces. Women high schoolers throw a 2 pound, 3½ ounce discus. In college competition, the discus weighs 2 kilograms, almost 4½ pounds, for both men and women.

The discus is thrown from a circle that is 8'2½" in diameter. It must land in a throwing sector that is formed by two lines extending outward from the center of the circle at a 45-degree angle. You are not permitted to step outside the throwing circle at any time; do so, and it's a foul.

When you grip and throw the discus, you want to make it travel high in the air but also parallel to the ground for as much of its flight as possible. And you want to make it spin like a Frisbee as it soars. You have to combine all of these characteristics—high and level flight, plus spin—in order to achieve good distance with your throws.

In gripping the discus, the first joint of each finger should overlap the disc edge. The thumb should rest on the discus back for added control, as should your palm and wrist.

Skilled and experienced discus throwers perform from 1½ to 2 full turns in the throwing circle in their effort to build up momentum and get distance into their throws. But as a beginner you should learn to release from a standing position before you begin attempting a step-and-turn delivery.

Stand with your left foot at the front of the throwing circle so your body is sideways to the direction in which you want the discus to go. Your feet should be about the width of your shoulders apart, which places your right foot close to the center of the ring.

Once you've adjusted your grip, swing the discus from left to right; swing it as far to the right as is comfortable. Then swing it back and forth one or two more times. You're winding up for the throw.

When you bring the discus across your body to release it,

In the discus grip, fingertips overlap the rim.

it's your right foot that triggers the action. Push off from your right foot, straightening the right leg, and rotate the right hip toward the direction of the throw. Then the right arm swings through, following an upward plane. Release the discus at about shoulder level. Follow through, continuing your arm swing and the rotation of your hips.

What's important to understand is that your throwing arm, the shoulder, and the discus always trail your turning body. As you approach the point of release, your arm whips through, uncoiling like a spring. Be sure to perfect this aspect of the delivery and release before you seek to add steps and a turn to your delivery.

The object of the turn, of course, is to build momentum and then impart that momentum to the discus as it is released. Try a delivery that involves a turn and a half. Take your stance at the rear of the throwing circle, your back to the direction of your throw. Your feet should be about shoulder width apart, your weight evenly distributed on the balls of your feet.

Begin your windup by swinging the discus back and forth in front of your body once or twice. Keep your feet stationary. When you begin your delivery, develop your turning speed gradually, so that at the end of the turn you and the discuss are approaching maximum speed. Then you whip the discus away.

When your weight is concentrated on your right foot and the discus is far to the right, the throw begins. Your left arm and shoulder lead the way. Shift your weight to your left foot and pivot around on it. As you pivot, your right leg swings wide. Land on the ball of your right foot, and then pivot around on *it*. You've now completed a 360-degree turn, and your back is again facing toward the direction of your throw.

All the while, your right arm and shoulder—and the discus—are trailing the movement of your lower body.

Now you're poised for the final phase of your delivery, the one-half turn that ends in the release. As your body continues to pivot on the ball of your right foot, your left leg drives around. Put your left foot to the ground near the front

In winding up, swing the discus as far to the right as you can.

Here's a full view of the right-foot pivot.

Pivoting on the left foot, you land on the right, then pivot around on it.

of the throwing circle and brake your momentum with your left leg. It's at this instant that you must whip your right arm and shoulder forward, releasing the discus just above the level of your shoulder.

The final move as you follow through is to bring the right leg around and plant your right foot. This prevents you from overstepping the throwing circle.

As with the shot put, what you have to strive for is a delivery that is smooth and rhythmic. It's important to be fast as you spin about, otherwise spinning won't do you much good, but it's more important to have a delivery that's well-timed, well co-ordinated. Your technique in this regard should be the focal point of your training program.

A final word about throwing accuracy: The discus will travel in the direction your left foot is pointed when you plant it just before the release. So take great care as to how you

In final phase, right arm and shoulder whip the discus away.

plant it. You can work to improve your accuracy by setting out a target—a towel, for instance—and aiming for it as you release, remembering to plant the left foot so it points in the direction of the target. When you're competing, imagine the towel is still there.

In practice sessions, work on both standing and throwing, and turning and throwing, but not any more than two or three times a week. Wind sprints, stretching exercises, calisthenics, and perhaps some weight training should also be included in your program.

13

The Javelin

"The javelin throw is a body throw and a leg throw," Mark Murro of Arizona State University, the first American to exceed the 300-foot mark, once remarked. "What you want is a fast run, then a good left-foot plant. You stop the body's momentum and transfer that momentum to your throwing arm."

Most javelin specialists are tall athletes, trimly built, with long legs and long arms. But you don't necessarily have to be taller than average to do well in the event. Finland's Jorma Kinnunen, who once held the world record with a throw of 304'1½", stood a mere 5'6" and weighted 160 pounds.

The javelin can be made of wood or metal, but it is always metal tipped. In both high school and college competition, it has these specifications.

	WEIGHT	LENGTH
Women	600 gm. (1 lb., 5.16 oz.)	220 cm.–230 cm. (7'2½"–7'6½")
Men	800 gm. (1 lb., 12.2 oz.)	260 cm.–270 cm. (8'6¼"–10¼")

Halfway up the javelin shaft, there's a cord grip. The javelin cannot be held at any other part of the shaft, according to the rules.

Terri Tupper
U.S. Military Academy
Women's javelin champion (159'1"), Penn Relays, 1979

Develop your technique, first. Unfortunately, there's a dearth of coaches, so as an alternative get a good instruction book and study the sequence pictures carefully. Everytime you prepare to throw, think of what the perfect throw looks like; think of what your body should be doing.

You also should develop your general strength by lifting weights. Pullovers and wrist curls, triceps extensions, and biceps extensions are some of the exercises you should be doing. Leg presses are good, too. If you don't have a coach to advise you, consult a book on strength training. There are several good ones available. Always have a spotter with you when you're working with weights.

A javelin costs about $75. A good one will last you several years.

The approach runway is 4 meters in width. At the end of the runway, there's a scratch line. Your foot cannot touch or go beyond the line.

The throwing sector is formed by two lines extending at a 30-degree angle from a point 8 meters behind the scratch line. Throws are measured from the point where the javelin first touches to the scratch line.

Hold the javelin high; accelerate gradually as you run.

There are several gripping styles, but the one beginners usually use involves placing the javelin diagonally across the palm, so the middle finger hooks around the back end of the cord winding. The index finger either coils around the shaft or simply lies parallel to it. Use whichever style feels the most comfortable.

The rules of the event require than the javelin be thrown from the shoulder. You are not permitted to sling the javelin as one does the discus.

Speed and accuracy are what are important. You achieve speed by virtue of your approach, making your strides faster and faster as you go, and then transferring that approach speed to the javelin as you release it.

But before you try a running approach, practice throwing the javelin from a standing position. In these drills, concentrate on aligning the javelin with the direction of the the throw. Also concentrate on getting a flat trajectory. Generally speaking, the flatter the trajectory, the farther the implement will travel.

Stand sideways to the direction of the throw, keeping your feet about shoulder width apart. Your left foot should point in the direction of the throw, while your right foot should be a few inches to the right of the direction of the throw.

You're going to throw the javelin overhand, the elbow leading as the throwing arm swings through. As you take the javelin back, concentrate your weight on your right leg. Extend the right arm to its full length. Extend your left arm for balance. Keep your upper body erect, your chin up, your eyes focused in the horizon. The tip of the javelin should be at about eye level.

Shifting your weight from your right leg to your left, start

In the final stages of approach, you execute a cross-step to get your body in position for the throw.

the javelin forward. Your hips come square to the direction of the throw. Be sure to use an over-the-shoulder motion, the elbow leading. Snap the wrist as you release.

When you feel you're ready to try a running approach, map out one that is 8 or 10 strides in length. An experienced javelin thrower is likely to use a 12- or 14-step approach.

No matter the number of strides you take, begin slowly, gradually increasing your speed as you go. Carry the javelin high in the air, keeping your wrist cocked. Your grip doesn't have to be tight at this stage.

The last few steps of the approach are crucial. As you enter the final stage, take the javelin back until your right arm is fully extended behind you. Tilt your upper body back. Tighten your grip.

To get your body into a throwing position without losing any momentum, you must execute a smooth cross-step with your right foot as you approach the point of release. Start pivoting your body for the execution of this cross-step at a point 5 strides from the point of release.

Following the cross-step, your left foot hits the ground just behind the scratch line and brakes to stop your forward thrust. Now the throwing arm and shoulder whip forward. Come straight over the shoulder with the javelin. The cross-step puts the body into a throwing position. The braking action of the left foot helps to get the entire body into the throw.

Your right leg swings forward, the right foot preventing you from going over the scratch line.

Most competitors in this event establish two checkpoints. One is placed at the start, the other where the final phase of the approach begins, 5 steps from the point of release.

Training for this event should include standing throws and running throws, the last named with run-ups of only 5 or 6 strides. This drill enables you to concentrate on getting your body in the correct throwing position before the release. Because the approach is an abbreviated one, you won't wear yourself out.

Jogging and sprint work are also recommended. These

help to increase your approach speed.

Since success in javelin throwing involves the muscles of the upper body and throwing arm to a great extent, weight training programs to strengthen these muscles are often prescribed. Consult your coach about such a program.

Throwing motion is directly overhead.

14

The Hammer Throw

The hammer throw is, like the shot put, an event in which strength is the vital factor, but quickness and a keen sense of balance are important, too. As of 1980, at least, American women did not officially compete in this event.

The implement used in the hammer throw consists of a metal ball—resembling a shot—that is linked to a grip by a thin steel wire, 4' long. The high school hammer weighs 12 pounds; it's 16 pounds in college competition.

The hammer is hurled for distance from within a throwing circle that is 7 feet in diameter. There is no stopboard at the front of the circle. The hammer must land in a throwing sector formed by two lines extending at a 45-degree angle from the center of the circle. You are not permitted to step upon or over the circle as you wind up to throw.

You wear leather gloves, padded to protect the fingers, in this event. When you take your grip, position the hammer handle across the middle fingers of your right hand. The left hand goes over the right, covering it. Keep both hands relaxed as you grip.

The distance you achieve with your throw depends on how much speed you are able to develop in the hammer head as you whirl it about. Begin by learning how to throw from a

The hammer — a metal ball linked to a steel handle by a 4-foot length of wire.

You need gloves for this event. When gripping, left hand goes over right.

standing-still position. Stand at the back of the throwing circle with your feet about shoulder width apart, your back to the direction of the throw. The ball should be behind you and within the circle. Turn your body to the right and bend your left knee as you grasp the handle. Your left arm should then form a straight line with the hammer cable.

Pulling the hammer with your left arm and shoulder, sweep it into the air over your head, your arms and upper body rotating as you swing. Keep your feet fixed to where you're standing. Bend your knees slightly. Your arms should be straight and relaxed. The hammer should trail your arms slightly as you swing. If you make the low point of each of the hammer's revolutions as far to your right as possible, it will make it easier for you to keep your arms ahead of the ball. After two or three turns, which should be enough to enable you to generate maximum momentum, lock your left leg and release.

To develop the greatest possible momentum, skilled and experienced throwers wind up by making several full turns within the circle before they release. The footwork involved in turning, however, is not easy to master. That's the chief reason that you should become adept at throwing from a standing position before you try turning and throwing.

Manny Silverio
Manhattan College

National AAU Junior Champion, 1976
IC4A Champion, 1979 (198'7")

A young teen-ager beginning this event should concentrate on his footwork, on the turns, without any hammer. And he should be certain he's in good condition. Running is more important than weight lifting at this stage. Once he's skilled in the turns, he can start working out with a lightweight hammer, one in which the ball weighs 4 pounds or so, and then slowly begin working his way up to a hammer of standard weight.

Begin with the ball in the ring behind you.

Sweep it into the air over your head.

You have to execute each turn as fast and efficiently as possible. Think of what a spinning top looks like. It rotates with its greatest speed when it spins on a perfectly vertical plane and while fixed to its balancing point. But it starts slowing down when it tilts in one direction or the other. As a hammer thrower, you have to imitate the twirling top, spinning fast while in an upright position and within as small a space as possible.

Advanced throwers take 3 or 4 full turns before releasing, pulling the hammer to its low point and being pulled by *it* to its high point on each turn. The footwork is quick and light, and accelerates with each turn.

Before you think of taking 3 or 4 turns, try just 1, preceding the turns with two full swings of the hammer from a standing-still position, keeping your arms as straight as possible. As you're completing the second swing and the hammer passes its lowest point, start to swivel on the heel of your left foot and the toe of the right. Then pick up your right foot, having shifted your weight to the left, and cross it in front of the left. You've now made one half of your turn. Continue spinning. When the right foot lands, you'll again be facing the back of the circle. Brake with the left foot. Lock the left leg and release.

As you add another turn, and then a third, your footwork is the same, with the finish of one turn putting you in a position to begin the next. Remember, each turn must be faster than the one previous. Your arms should be fully extended as you turn, with your arms and upper body always moving ahead of the ball. Your knees should be bent throughout, but straighten at the moment of release as you lift with your legs, pulling the hammer from its low point, catapulting it into the air.

This is not an event that every athlete should try. You have to have a well-muscled body but at the same time be quick on your feet. The hammer throw takes the right outlook, too. Most hammer throwers work a long time before

Footwork in turning; begin by facing away from the direction of the throw; pivot on the left heel, then cross the right foot in front of the left. Keep spinning. Your feet end up in the same position as when you started.

they begin to make any real progress, so patience is a good quality to have.

You also have to have the opportunity to work closely with a coach to develop the proper throwing technique. A supervised weight training program is another must.

Your arms should be fully extended as you release.

Glossary

Achilles tendon: The tendon at the back of the heel that joins the heel bone and the calf muscles.

Age-group competition: Competition in which those entered compete in categories according to their ages.

Amateur Athletic Union (AAU): The ruling body of track and field in the United States. It conducts national and regional championships and organizes teams that represent the U.S. in international competition, including the Olympics.

Anchor leg: The final leg of a relay race.

Anchorman: The member of a relay team who is the last to compete in a race.

Approach: The run that precedes the takeoff in vaulting or jumping, or the run to the foul line in the javelin throw.

Association for Intercollegiate Athletics for Women (AIAW): The governing body of women's college sports.

Baton: A hollow, tubelike object, about a foot in length, made of wood, metal, or plastic, that is passed from one runner to another in a relay race.

Blind pass: In a sprint relay, a technique of passing the baton in which the receiver does not look at the incoming runner, but takes the baton on the basis of his sense of touch and the incoming runner's shouted command.

Blocks: See Starting blocks.

Box; box in: To surround and hem in a runner during the race, forcing him either to drop back or go to the outside to pass.

Broad jump: See Long jump.

Bunched start: In a sprint race, a start in which the blocks are so set that the toes of the rear foot are about 12 inches behind the toes of the front foot.

Cross country: Distance running over hills, unpaved roads, through wooded areas, or other variable terrain. Cross-country courses usually range from 2 to 6 miles in length.

Crossbar: The light bar of metal or wood, approximately 12 to 14 feet in length, that rests on pins or small supports extending from the pair of upright standards, and which must be cleared by high jumpers and pole vaulters in their events.

Cut to the pole: In a middle distance or distance race, to move toward the inside lane following a scratch start.

Dead heat: A race in which two or more competitors cross the finish line exactly the same time.

Dip finish: A tactic used by a runner as he approaches the tape in which he thrusts his arms to the rear, projecting his shoulders forward on a slightly downward plane into the tape.

Dual meet: A track and field meet between two teams. Each team's score is the sum of the scores of the individual team members.

Elongated start: In a sprint race, a start in which the blocks are so set that the knee of the rear leg is next to the heel of the front foot.

Exchange zone: In relay races, a strip of the track 20 meters (22 yards) in length, and 1 lane in width, and within which the baton must be passed. Also called passing zone.

False start: Movement by a runner across the starting line or off the blocks before the starting signal is given. There is no penalty for one false start; for two, however, a competitor can be disqualified.

Fartlek training: A method of building one's endurance in which the runner alternates periods of sprinting with those of easy running or jogging over cross-country terrain. The word "fartlek" is Swedish and means "speed play."

Field: The total number of runners in a race.

Finish tape: See Tape.

Flats: Lightweight training shoes without any spikes.

Float: To run at top speed with less than a full effort.

Flop: A technique of high jumping in which the jumper goes over the bar backwards and headfirst and lands on his back.

Fosbury Flop: See Flop.

Gather: To increase one's arm and leg action as the finish of the race approaches.

Gun lap: The final lap of a distance race; the firing of a pistol signals the beginning of the lap.

Hamstring: Any of the tendons at the back of the knee.

Hang: In the long jump, a technique of using one's body in the air in which the trailing leg is brought alongside the lead leg. The body remains suspended in this manner until just before the landing when the legs are kicked forward.

Heat: See Trial heat.

High hurdles: A race run over hurdles that are 39 inches high (in high school competition) and 42 inches high (in college competition). A common indoor distance is 60 yards (5 hurdles); common outdoor distances are 110 meters and 120 yards (10 hurdles).

Hitch-kick: In the running long jump, a technique of using one's body in the air on which a stride and a half are taken before the feet are brought together in preparation for the landing.

Hop, step, and jump: See Triple jump.

Hurdle: A wooden or metal barrier over which hurdlers must jump in hurdle races.

Intercollegiate Association of Amateur Athletics of America (IC4A): A track and field organization made up of Eastern colleges; conducts annual championship meet.

Intermediate hurdles: A race run over hurdles that are 36 inches in height. A common distance in high school competition is 330 yards (8 hurdles).

Interval training: A training technique that involves alternating sprinting and jogging over set distances.

Invitational meet: A track and field meet to which the promoter invites all participants.

Kick: A runner's burst of speed near the end of a race.

Lap: One complete circuit of a track: also, to overtake and increase one's lead over a competitor by a full circuit of the track.

Layout: That part of the high jump between the takeoff and landing during which the jumper is clearing the crossbar, his body in generally a horizontal position.

Lead leg: In hurdling, the leg that goes first over the hurdle.

Leg: A portion of a relay race that each member of a team must run.

Long distance: A race from 1,500 meters (1 mile) through the marathon (26 miles, 385 yards).

Long jump: A field event in which each competitor leaps for distance from a running start; also called a broad jump or running long jump.

Low hurdles: A race run over hurdles that are 30 inches in height. A common outdoor distance in high school competition is 180 yards (8 hurdles).

Marathon: A race over a course that measures 26 miles, 385 yards.

Medium start: In a sprint race, a start in which the blocks are so set that the knee of the rear leg is next to the toes of the front foot.

Medley relay: A relay race in which the various legs are of uneven lengths.

Middle distance: A race of 40 meters (440 yards); 800 meters (880 yards).

National Collegiate Athletic Association (NCAA): The ruling body of college track and field (as well as other sports) for men in the United States.

Open meet: A track meet that is not restricted to any particular class of competitors.

Pace: The speed at which a race is run or the speed of the leader in a race.

Pass: In relay races, the exchange of the baton from one runner to another.

Passing zone: See Exchange zone.

Preliminary heat: See Trial heat.

Put: To propel the shot in the shot-put event by extending the arm back, then straightening it so the shot is thrust into the air from the shoulder.

Recall: To call back the runners just after the start of a race because of a false start.

Relay: A race between teams, usually with four members to a team, that is run in four stages, called legs. Each member of each team runs one leg.

Rolling start: An illegal start in which a competitor raises from his "set" position in anticipation of the firing of the starter's gun.

Running long jump: See Long jump.

Runway: In such events as the high jump and pole vault, the area or path used in the approach.

Scissors: A method of high jumping in which the lead leg clears the bar while the jumper is in a sitting position; the trailing leg is then snapped over.

Scratch line: In the long jump, high jump, and javelin throw, a line over which a competitor must not step in order to have his jump or throw qualify for measurement.

Scratch start: A start in which the runners line up in a straight line across the track, as in the mile run. There is no adjusting of the runners starting points. Runners, however, are permitted to "cut to the pole" after reaching the first turn.

Shin splint: Pain and swelling in the shin, the result of muscle inflammation.

Spikes: Low cut, lightweight track shoes with nail-like or cone-shaped projections fitted to the sole, or sole and heel; used by sprinters for fast starts and surer footing.

Splits: The measured times for a runner at specific intervals in a distance race; for example, every 100 meters in a 400-meter race.

Sprint: Any race up to 200 meters (220 yards).

Staggered start: A start of a race in which competitors are assigned starting points that serve to compensate for the unequal distance each is to run. The starting point for each lane from the inside to outside is progressively farther ahead.

Starter: The official responsible for the start of the race. He fires the starting gun and calls false starts.

Starting blocks: Adjustable supports mounted on either side of a metal frame than enable a runner to brace his feet at the start of a sprint race.

Stopboard: See Toeboard.

Straddle: A technique of high jumping in which the jumper crosses the bar stomach down and parallel to it, the legs apart.

Straightaway: The straight part of a track between curves.

Takeoff board: In the long jump and triple jump, a rectangular board set into the ground from which the jumper drives in making his jump.

Take-off box: See Vaulting box.

Tape: The length of string or yard stretched across the track four or five feet immediately above the finish line that aids the officials in determining the winner of a race. Also called finish tape.

Throwing circle: In certain field events, such as the shot put and discus throw, a circular area within which the competitor must remain during his or her throwing attempt.

Throwing sector: In the shot put, discus, and javelin throws, the area in which the object thrown must land in order to be qualified as a legal throw.

Timer: One of several officials responsible for timing runners' speeds during a race.

Toeboard: A curved board, 4 inches high, 4 feet long, secured to the front edge of the throwing circle in the shot put to help prevent competitors from overstepping the circle. Also called a stopboard.

Trial heat: One of two or more preliminary contests held to eliminate competitors from a final contest in which there are too many entrants to compete at one time. Also called preliminary heat.

Triple jump: A field event in which each competitor jumps for distance from a running start, landing first on the takeoff foot (a hop), then on the other foot (a step), and, last, on both feet (a jump). Formerly called the hop, step, and jump.

Vaulting box: In the pole vault, a rectangular opening with a slanted bottom in which the pole is planted at the beginning of a vault. Also called a takeoff box.

Visual pass: In relay races, a baton exchange in which the receiver watches the incoming runner as the pass is being made. Visual passes are common to distance races, not sprints.

Warm down: A period of light exercise, such as jogging, by which a competitor seeks to relax and recover from hard exercise.

Warm up: A period of increasingly strenuous exercise designed to loosen muscles and increase the rate of blood circulation before hard exercise or competition.

Western roll: A method of high jumping in which the jumper goes over the bar while lying on his side, and often with the trailing leg tucked under the lead leg.

APPENDIX I

Track and Field Organizations

Road Runners Club of America (RRCA)
2737 Devonshire Pl., N.W.
Washington, DC 20008

Amateur Athletic Union (AAU)
AAU House
3400 West 86 St.
Indianapolis, IN 46268

U.S. Track and Field Federation (USTFF)
30 N. Norton Ave.
Tucson, AZ 85719

Association for Intercollegiate Athletics for Women (AIAW)
1201 16th St., NW
Washington, D.C. 20036

National Collegiate Athletic Association (NCAA)
349 East Thomas Rd.
Phoenix, AZ 85012

High School Records

Girls' Track and Field

100-yard dash	10.3	M. Gillette; Park Forest, Illinois	1967
220-yard dash	23.3	Chandra Cheeseborough; Jacksonville, Florida	1977
440-yard dash	54.2	Merry Johnson; Canyon, Texas	1977
880-yard run	2:07.7	Delisa Walton; Detroit, Michigan	1978
1-mile run	4:43.1	Julie Shea; Raleigh, North Carolina	1977
2-mile run	10.12.5	Martha Wright; State College, Pennsylvania	1978
50-yard hurdles	6.7	Gail Boyd; Lebannon, Oregon	1966
80-yard hurdles	10.1	Yvonne Boone; Oakland, California	1975
High Jump	6'1"	Sharon Burrill; Denver Colorado	1978
Long Jump	22'1¾"	Kathy McMillan; Raeford, North Carolina	1976
Triple Jump	40'¼"	Easter Barbel; Houston, Texas	1978
Shot Put (8 lbs.)	48'8½"	Dottie Barnes; Gresham, Oregon	1971
Discus	161'11"	Helene Connell; Jackson, New Jersey	1977
Javelin	165'5"	Kitsy Hall; Rogue River, Oregon	1976

High School Records

Boys' Track and Field

100-yard dash	9.0	Houston McTear; Baker, Florida	1975
220-yard dash	20.5	Dwayne Evans; Phoenix, Arizona	1976
440-yard dash	45.8	Ronald Ray; Newport News, Virginia	1972
880-yard dash	1:48.8	Richard Joyce; Whittier, California	1965
1-mile run	3:58.3	James Ryun; Wichita Kansas	1965
120-yard high hurdles	12.9	Renaldo Nehemiah; Scotch Plains, New Jersey	1977
180-yard low hurdles	18.1	Steve Caminiti; Encino, California	1964
330-yard Int. hurdles	35.9	William Blessing; Dallas, Texas	1974
High Jump	7'4¼"	Gail Olsen; Sycamore, Illinois	1978
Long Jump	24'0"	Michael Lee; Columbus, Ohio	1978
Triple Jump	52'6¼"	David Rucker; Fresno, California	1970
Pole Vault	17'4¼"	Anthony Curran; Ventura, California	1978
Shot Put (12 lbs.)	72'3¼"	Sam Walker; Dallas, Texas	1978
Discus	207'8"	Scott Crowell; Mason City, Iowa	1978
Javelin	254'11"	Russell Francis; Pleasant Hill, Oregon	1971

Metric Conversion Tables-1

Track Events

METERS	MILES	YARDS	FEET	INCHES
1	0	1	0	3.37
2	0	2	0	6.74
3	0	3	0	10.11
4	0	4	1	1.48
5	0	5	1	4.85
10	0	10	2	9.70
20	0	21	2	7.40
30	0	32	2	5.10
40	0	43	2	2.80
50	0	54	2	.50
60	0	65	1	10.20
70	0	76	1	7.90
80	0	87	1	5.60
90	0	98	1	3.30
100	0	109	1	1.00
110	0	120	0	10.70
200	0	218	2	2.00
300	0	328	0	3.00
400	0	437	1	4.00
500	0	546	2	5.00
1,000	0	1,093	1	10.00
1,500	0	1,640	1	3.00
2,000	1	427	0	8.00
2,500	1	974	0	1.00
3,000	1	1,520	2	6.00
5,000	3	188	0	2.00
10,000	6	376	0	4.00

APPENDIX III
Metric Conversion Tables-2

Track Events

Yards	Meters
40	36.58
50	45.72
60	54.86
70	64.01
75	68.58
100	91.44
110	100.58
120	109.73
220	201.17
300	274.32
440	402.34
600	548.64
880	804.67
1,000	914.40
1,320	1,207.01

Metric Conversion Tables-3

Track Events

MILES	KILOMETERS
1	1.6093
2	3.2187
3	4.8280
4	6.4374
5	8.0467
6	9.6561
7	11.2654
8	12.8748
9	14.4841
10	16.0935

Metric Conversion Tables-4

Field Events

FEET	METERS
1	.305
2	.610
3	.914
4	1.219
5	1.524
6	1.829
7	2.134
8	2.438
9	2.743
10	3.048
20	6.096
30	9.144
40	12.192
50	15.240
60	18.288
70	21.336
80	24.384
90	27.432
100	30.480
200	60.960

Author Bio

A full-time free-lance author, **GEORGE SULLIVAN** has written a good-sized shelf of books.

He was born in Massachusetts where he attended public schools. From 1945–48, he served in the Navy, working as a journalist. He then went on to Fordham University, graduating with a B.S. degree in 1952. Before turning to free-lance writing, he worked as a public relations manager for AMF. He is a member of the Authors Guild and the American Society of Journalists and Authors.

Mr. Sullivan lives in New York City with his wife and son, Timothy.

Index